A MIRACLE A MINUTE

**With Candle Burning Prayers
For a Good and Prosperous Life**

by

Arthur Crockett and Maria D'Andrea

Interior Art Work by Lorenzo Southerland

Front Cover Graphic by F fang/Dreamstime.com

LET THERE BE LIGHT

A MIRACLE A MINUTE
With Candle Burning Prayers
For a Good and Prosperous Life
by
Arthur Crockett and Maria D' Andrea

Published in the United States of America By
Timothy G. Beckley dba Inner Light / Global Communications
Box 753 · New Brunswick, NJ 08903

Staff Members
Timothy G. Beckley, Publisher
Carol Ann Rodriguez, Assistant to the Publisher
Sean Casteel, General Associate Editor
Tim R. Swartz, Graphics and Editorial Consultant
William Kern, Editorial and Art Consultant

Sign Up On The Web For Our Free Weekly Newsletter
and Mail Order Version of Conspiracy Journal
and Bizarre Bazaar
www.Conspiracy Journal.com

Order Hot Line: 1-732-602-3407
PayPal: MrUFO8@hotmail.com

CONTENTS

A MIRACLE A MINUTE
By Arthur Crockett

RETURN FROM THE DEAD
VISIONS OF HEAVEN, HELL AND THE ANGELS

Ever since St. Paul saw a vision of Jesus Christ in the desert during his death experience, man has had similar visions during moments when death seemed only moments away.

Usually, we are not so privileged. Nearly all death experiences from which people return are exactly alike. They speak of an extremely intense light, or of a dark tunnel. Friends and relatives long dead appear to them. Sometimes they are shocked to find someone who they did not think of as dead, someone they thought was alive. In many cases the dying person sees the great light and has a compulsion to go to it. In other cases the person is told to go back, that it is not time for him to pass over.

In one recent case a young man in New York City was stabbed and was close to death. Paramedics and doctors worked over him feverishly and miraculously brought him back to the world of the living. The young man then related a strange experience. He said that while he was unconscious he saw his dead brother who had died a year earlier. The brother told him, "Go back! We don't have room for you! Go back!" The young man was aware of hands pushing him away from the area he was in while unconscious. And the area?

Was it Heaven or simply another plane of existence? Even the young man doesn't know. He was aware only of his dead brother, seeing him exactly as he did in life, solid, three dimensional.

No, we all don't see visions of the Holy Family when we are

near death. As we said earlier, only a very few are so privileged. However, there are those who see those benign entities we like to call our guardian angels.

THE LILLY EXPERIENCE

In his autobiography, John Lilly relates a powerful near-death experience. Lilly was best known for his scientific research with dolphins. His book, *"The Center of the Cyclone,"* tells about his meeting with two guardian angels.

He reports that the entities offered him warmth, "and were conveyed to him in a series of reverential, awesome thoughts."

Lilly was instructed by the angels in a number of spiritual matters, and he says:

"They say they are my guardian angels, that they have been with me before at critical times and that in fact they are with me always, but I am not usually in a state to perceive when I am close to the death of the body."

Lilly gives some insight into the nature of such guardians in another paragraph:

"Their magnificent deep powerful love overwhelms me to a certain extent, but I finally accept it. As they move closer, I find less and less of me and more and more of them in my being. They stop at a critical distance and say to me that this time I have developed only to the point where I can stand their presence at this particular distance. If they came any closer, they would overwhelm me and I would lose myself as a cognitive entity, merging with them. They further say that I separated them into two, because that is my way of perceiving them, but that in reality they are one in the space in which I found myself. They say that I insist on still being an individual, forcing a projection onto them, as if they were two. They further communicate to me that if I go back to my body as I developed further, I would eventually perceive the oneness of them, and of me, and of many others."

Apparently, guardian angels (or angel) had a power that we mortals know nothing about. We can see that they did not want Lilly to get too close to them, or run the risk of being overwhelmed. Yet, the phenomenon is not unique.

THE DIOTTO EXPERIENCE

Angelo Diotto of Padua, Italy was 10 years old when he nearly drowned in a swimming pool. After his recovery he spoke of his experiences with someone who called himself a guardian angel.

It was July 10, 1968. Angelo was not an especially religious boy. He avoided going to church whenever possible and was considered quite mischievous. He was devil-may-care and, in fact, it was this lack of fear that had gotten him into trouble in the swimming pool. He had been warned to stay away from the deep end of the pool because he did not know how to swim. But he jumped in, anyway, and nearly drowned.

When lifesavers brought him around, the boy said that he had heard wonderful music in the water, and that when he felt hands pulling him to the surface, he did not want to go.

Angelo told his listeners that after the first few seconds of panic, he did not want to be saved. He said, "I saw things I had never seen before. They were wonderful. A man spoke to me and said he was my guardian angel and that he was always watching over me, but that I made it difficult for him because I was mischievous.

"I wanted to run to him but he held up both hands and told me to stand still. He said I should not get too close to him because I was not ready yet, that I would be returning to the land of the living. He said it was dangerous for me to be too near him.

"Then he started to fade away. Everything became a blur and all of a sudden I was lying on the ground and my mother was crying and men kept pushing some kind of cone onto my face."

The Lilly experience concerning the guardian angels' insistence that he not get too close was repeated with the Diotto experi-

ence. And it is seen again and again with the near-death experiences of others who have seen and talked to angels who are guardians or guides to the living.

What is this mystical power? No one knows. What we do know is that in every case of near-death in which angels or the Holy Family is involved, there is distance between the subject and the vision. There is always distance between those who have visions in a walking state on earth and the entity being envisioned. In no case on record has anyone seeing a vision been close enough to touch the hem of the garment of the angel, or any member of the Holy Family. Even St. Paul in the desert, when he saw Christ, was not at all close to Jesus.

VISIONS OF HEAVEN

There is never a shortage of critics who insist that the near-death vision of Heaven is nothing more than an hallucination. Naturally, we can't be sure that what is reported to us by those who have almost passed over is true. But those who have seen what it is like on the other side are so convincing that one tends to believe, even if one is a hard-headed realist. The point at which most staunch critics fall apart in their derision is when the near-death individual states that since he or she has seen what is waiting ahead, *there is no longer any fear of death.*

Probably the most ancient report comes from Stephen, whose death by stoning is recorded in the Bible, Acts 7: 54-9.

"Now when they heard these things they were enraged, and they ground their teeth against him. But he (Stephen) full of the Holy Spirit, gazed into heaven and said, 'Behold, I see the heavens open up, and the Son of man standing at the right hand of God.' But they cried out with a loud voice and stopped their ears and rushed upon him. Then they cast him out of the city and stoned him. And as they were stoning Stephen he prayed, 'Lord Jesus, receive my spirit.'"

In our own generation we have a report from a writer in Johnson City, Kansas. He wrote: "Last night my wife and I were visit-

ing across the street. We talked about writing because our hostess has written many books, and I told her I was writing one, too, and that I was about to start one on death-bed visions.

"My hostess said that when she was younger she went to see her grandmother, who lay dying. She was so still and quiet on the bed that everyone in the room thought she was dead. But she wasn't. She sat up suddenly and looked around. The old woman was quite annoyed that she was still alive.

"When her annoyance passed, she told the group that she already had a peek over the wall and described it like a park more lovely than anything she had ever seen or imagined. She also talked about hearing music that was like a great symphony of voices. According to the old woman, it was more pleasing to the ear than anything she had ever heard on earth.

"She made no bones about how disappointed she was when she opened her eyes and saw her family hovering over her bed. The old woman said that she was anxious to return to the heavenly glory that awaited her on the other side. She wanted to explore what she had seen. She wanted to be there to hear that music.

"My hostess said that her grandmother said nothing about meeting anyone she knew on the other side. She saw only what she perceived as heaven, and heard only heavenly voices."

We can conclude from this that not all experiences are the same. The old woman's awareness began with a view of the countryside; others on the threshold of death don't see the countryside, but do see those who have departed before them.

CHILDREN'S VISIONS OF HEAVEN

Dr. Harold Paul Sloan told incidents of children's deaths. He reported them on a Philadelphia radio station in 1943. In one case there was two-year-old Florence Repp, who lay dying in her grandmother's arms. The little girl appeared to be listening to something. Then she said, "Music! Grandma, hear the music?"

The woman replied that she didn't hear anything.

Little Florence said, "Shush! It's music! They're playing up there!"

The girl died seconds later.

Dr. Sloan also told about the two-year-old mongoloid child of Roy Rogers and Dale Evans. On the day of little Robin's funeral the child's nurse told Dale Evans:

"All day Sunday Robin was unconscious, her eyes closed. Well, just a few seconds before she died, she opened her eyes real wide. Then she lifted both her little hands toward the ceiling and smiled radiantly, just as if she knew where she was going and was glad. I've heard of such things happening, Dale, but in all my years of nursing this is the first time I've ever seen it. And I'm sure your baby met our Lord. I saw it happen!"

In another remarkable case, 12-year-old Lowell Jones lost his speech toward the end of his short life on earth. His mother had died years before. Moments before death took him, he raised his arms and cried, "Oh, Mother!" It was as though he had found her in the next world.

Famed Washington correspondent Ruth Montgomery told a rather startling story about a six-week-old baby boy who was born with a defective heart. The boy's mother told Montgomery, "Suddenly, our little baby, who was lying in his crib, sat up all by himself and looked straight at me. I was terribly shaken, not only because I had never heard of so young a baby raising and holding himself erect, but because of the unfathomable look in his big blue eyes. It was an other-world gaze, wise, adult, which plainly told me that he was not going to live, and that I was not to grieve."

IS HEAVEN 1,000 MILES UP?

Silly question? On the surface, it would appear so. Yet an out-of-body experience felt by the noted psychoanalyst Carl Jung does cause one to wonder.

Jung had broken his foot and had then suffered a severe heart attack. He lingered between life and death for a long time. During this period he had a series of nightly visions. Fortunately, he wrote them down as they occurred, usually when he had enough strength to hold a pen.

One near-death out-of-body experience was reported this way: "Once it seemed to me that I was high up in space. Far below I saw the globe of earth, bathed in a glorious blue light. In many places the globe seemed colored, or spotted dark green like oxidized silver. Far away to the left lay a broad expanse the reddish-yellow desert of Arabia. Then it was as though the silver of the earth had assumed a reddish-gold hue. Beyond was the Red Sea and far back as if in the upper left of a map, I could just make out a bit of the Mediterranean."

Jung's estimation was that he was 1,000 miles out in space. He would have to be, he contended, to have that sort of view of the earth. He said later, "It is impossible to convey the beauty and intensity of emotion during those visions. They were the most tremendous things I have ever experienced.

"I would never have imagined that any such experience was possible. It was not a product of my imagination. The visions and experiences were utterly real; there was nothing subjective about them; they had a quality of absolute objectivity."

Carl Jung did not mention anything about seeing long-dead friends and relatives. He did not dwell on his own surroundings out there in space. And we wonder why his trip stopped at 1,000 miles. Was he on his way to heaven, but too awed by the sight of our globe to continue? Our own astronauts have seen the earth from greater distances and are equally awed by the sight. Were they nearer to heaven than we are because they traveled in space? The learned opinion is that we approach heaven only at death, or near-death, and that the exact location of the Paradise we speak of as heaven is not really known...except to the dead.

We can never be sure that man's death-bed visions of heaven

are true sightings. To understand the reasoning behind this we have to return to the Apostle Paul and his account of being taken to the Third Heaven.

Paul, who was earlier known as Saul, was born in Tarsus, a city in Asia Minor hundreds of miles from Palestine. His training was as a Pharisee, and he was a strict one. If you were to compare him to a man of today you would have to select a practical, down-to-earth lawyer, a no-nonsense individual who believed in the letter of the law.

That was Paul. Yet in Corinthians he wrote: "I know a man in Christ who fourteen years ago was caught up to the third heaven, whether in the body or out of the body I do not know, God knows. And I know that this man was caught up into paradise ...and heard things that cannot be told, which man may not utter."

Scholars agree that Paul was speaking of himself. What's more, he may have been the only one in history to have truly envisioned heaven.

VISIONS DURING GREAT DISASTERS

There are hundreds of stories of out-of-body experiences in which the dying later tell of seeing their own bodies on operating tables, or on floors while people work feverishly over them to bring life back. The dying tell us of their visions of the Holy Family, of angels, of Christ on the cross. However, it has also been shown that visions can occur to those who are threatened with disaster, especially when great masses of people are threatened by the same disaster. For instance, in April 1944 Englanders daily faced annihilation from Hitler's Luftwaffe. They had lived under the Nazis' bombs for five years and there seemed no end of to it.

On April 27 in Ipswich, during an air raid, hundreds of people saw a vision in the sky. It was Christ on the Cross. London newspapers carried the story and on May 7, the Chicago Tribune Press Service sent a dispatch which read in part:

"...numerous residents of eastern England stoutly maintain that

the sign of the cross was visible in the sky for fifteen minutes. Those who have given detailed descriptions include a naval commander, a carpenter, housewives, etc. The consensus of the statements is that the vision gradually grew clearer until the figure of Christ was distinct. The local pastor is investigating."

One eyewitness was William Garnham, an engineer. He said: "I saw the sign of the cross actually form. There was no mistake in either the shape of the crucifix or the figure nailed to it."

On May 8 the local pastor, Rev. Harold Godfrey Green, vicar of St. Nicholas Church and army chaplain, reported that he had interviewed 2,000 eyewitnesses. His conclusion was: "There was scarcely any variation—if any—in these accounts. I have verified the fact of the vision quite definitely. I am satisfied myself beyond doubt of the authenticity of the vision.

"There were clouds in the sky which drifted by while the vision remained stationary!"

History abounds in such cases. You can find numerous accounts of spiritual help coming to people in times of trouble. The Crusaders were sure they saw angelic hosts fighting for them on several occasions and the phantom horsemen came at a time when the Crusaders were certain they were about to be destroyed.

In the wars between the English and Scots, several cases of divine intervention were cited, and again during the Napoleonic wars. The most famous of all sightings, however, occurred during the latter part of August, 1914 over France.

So much first-hand and sincere testimony has been given that we can scarcely doubt the event. The occurrences were titled *"The Angels of Mons."* Again, one force of soldiers was threatened with annihilation by another. The British Army had 80,000 men in the field of Agincourt. They were opposed by 300,000 Germans who were backed up by terrific artillery fire.

During that period the Allies' dream of an early victory had been wiped out by the endlessly advancing Germans. Those were

the days of retreat, utter weariness, death and burning heat. But quite suddenly all of that was to change.

An eyewitness named Lance Corporal Headley-Johns of the Lancashire Fusiliers reported later: "I was with my battalion in the retreat from Mons on or about August 28. It was between eight and nine in the evening. I could see quite plainly in mid-air a strange light which seemed to be quite distinctly outlined and was not a reflection of the moon, nor were any clouds in the neighborhood.

"The light became brighter and I could see quite distinctly three shapes, one in the center having what looked like spread wings. The other two were not so large but quite plainly distinct from the center one. They appeared to have a long loose hanging garment of gold tint, and they were above the German lines and facing us.

"We stood watching them for about three quarters of an hour. All the men with me saw them, and other men came up from other groups who also told us they'd seen the same thing."

On the same night, August 28,1914, a wounded RAF man told nurse Phyllis Campbell: "We all saw it. First there was a yellowish mist sort of rising before the Germans as they came to the top of the hill. I just gave up. No use fighting the whole German race. The next minute, comes this funny cloud of light, and when it clears off there's a tall man with yellow hair and golden armor on a white horse, holding his sword up. Before you could take a breath, the Germans had turned and we were after them."

Captain Cecil Wightmick of the first corps British Intelligence witnessed the rout of the Germans. He said that the German infantry fled in panic and confusion, dropping their weapons and supplies and running like mad toward their homeland. Captain Wightmick learned later that the Germans had been shelling British machine gun nests when they suddenly shifted their fire to a deserted area. One British sergeant said in amazement, "Fritz has gone balmy. Why is he preparing that open ground?"

That, too, was explained when Captain Wightmick interrogated German prisoners. One said: "They were all clad in white. Mounted on white horses. We all saw them. We turned our big weapons and our machine gun on them, but they kept coming. The concentration of fire power was tremendous, but not a single white horseman fell."

The intervention of the "Angels" turned the tide of battle. The Allied position was no longer desperate.

VISIONS OF HELL

A study of both Testaments will not reveal the locations of heaven and hell. Both books are vague. And strangely enough, near-death experiences do include "hellish" insights. That is, a few who are saved from death will reveal during the process of being brought back to life that they have seen an ugliness that cannot be described. But when life is fully restored to these people, the visions that came to them are completely forgotten. There is no memory whatsoever. And perhaps that is as it should be.

Nevertheless, we are not completely in the dark about what hell really is. We get an inkling of what it is like from an attractive woman named Gloria Lee, who died in 1962 as a result of a fast that lasted too long. Shortly after her death a spiritual medium in Miami, Florida said that she had contacted Gloria and that Gloria said she would be in communication with someone in New Zealand.

The reason she selected someone so far away was because she wanted to make sure that person had no knowledge of Gloria Lee in life and would hold no prejudices.

Allegedly, Gloria contacted a medium in Auckland through automatic writing. A total of 35,000 words were recorded. Naturally, all of what she said can't be reprinted here, but it's interesting to note that her description of what is hell to her differs greatly from what we've been taught.

Gloria said, in part: "The glory was not yet because I first had to judge myself...It was then that I became aware of Cosmic Memory

...which registers with unfailing accuracy the thoughts and action of every living soul ...At a given moment after the entity leaves the earth, making the transition called death, the Cosmic Computer goes into action. It operates projector fashion, and is vividly clear and more beautifully colored than any mortal film.

"In my moment of truth it began to play back my life on earth, but in reverse. Therefore the first thing I saw quite clearly was my lifeless form surrounded by the grief auras of others. And that is the answer to the Day of Judgment. No Karmic Board, no Hierarchal Board, sits or stands sentinel. We are very alone in the moment of Truth.

"In what seemed to me to be a great, lonely vault of a place, I was watching a character called Gloria Lee going about her daily on the earth's plane. All the mannerisms I'd affected, the irritating habits I'd formed, were run off for me to see. But, from the new level, we are given a spiritual gift of judging what we have seen objectively, and such objectivity is razor sharp. Its immediate effect made me want to pare away the bruised parts of me that did not measure up to the Christ consciousness. To say it was an uncomfortable experience is to put it mildly. It can be downright agonizing to view yourself as others see you."

Is it hell to view yourself as others see you? We can't be sure. Hell is still elusive. We can be fairly certain that we don't burn in hell for an eternity. That punishment would be far too severe even for the most vile of criminals.

Yet the Bible tells us that there is a spiritual world of evil as well as a spiritual world of good. According to Matthew 25: 41, the former is occupied by "the devil and his angels." Included in this group are those who once served him in physical bodies, and who seek to seduce and possess men still on earth.

Superstition or fact? Take the teachings and example of Jesus Christ. His disciples were astonished to learn that they had the power to cast out demons. True, they did not always succeed, but the practice was continued for some time.

Somehow, the early church fell away from believing that demons existed. From time to time the church picked it up, but today demon possession is looked upon as nothing more than superstition.

Still, there are cases today which cannot be explained. Call them what you will, you will note that in every case reported here there were no deep, mysterious rituals involved in the casting out of the demons.

Not long ago a prominent Presbyterian minister in Korea was trying desperately to tell the story of Jesus to villagers who had never heard it before. He was not having much success because one woman in the group constantly interrupted him. It was obvious that the woman was insane.

Finally, the minister in total exasperation commanded in the name of Jesus Christ that the demon possessing the woman leave immediately. The woman went into convulsions, but minutes later when she recovered and she was completely sane. The minister finished his story.

In another case a medical doctor asked a Christian Scientist practitioner to help him with a woman patient who was a psychopathic killer. When the patient and the practitioner were left alone, the patient tried to choke her to death. Fortunately, the patient's daughter entered the room and stopped the attempted murder. The practitioner caught her breath, then exclaimed: "You devil, you get out of that woman and never bother her again!" A short time later the patient calmed down and began stroking the practitioner's hand. All evidence of psychopathic behavior in the woman was gone.

An even more startling case comes to us from a psychiatrist in the Middle West who has made a strange discovery. He prefers not to give his name, and you will understand why once you've heard his story. So far, he has told it only to the pastor of a large Congregational church.

The psychiatrist said he has had miraculous success with many

of his mental patients simply by commanding that the evil spirits leave in the name of Jesus Christ. He does it in the same way it was done shortly after Jesus told his disciples that it could be done.

The psychiatrist said that he does not dare tell his professional colleagues because he is afraid that they will think he is crazy. He told his pastor because he said he had to tell someone.

These cases of demon possession, and others, are the only glimpses we can have into the hell that surely must exist. It is quite possible that our sanity could not bear an actual vision of it.

THE MIRACLE AT FATIMA

We use the word "miracle" rather loosely. It was a miracle that we made it home before the downpour. It was a miracle that the baby was born on its mother's birthday. These, of course, are not true miracles. They are nothing more than coincidences. Our dictionaries describe a miracle as "an effect in the physical world which surpasses all known human or natural powers and is therefore subscribed as a supernatural agency."

Often, a true miracle is associated with the vision of the Holy Mother, or Jesus Christ, or Joseph. It makes sense that the Holy Family is not going to appear in earthly flesh simply for the sake of startling someone or filling him with awe. The reasons are often profound, sometimes mysterious, and sometimes unfathomable to our finite minds. However, the incredible incidents at Fatima leave no doubt in anyone's mind as to why the Holy Mother appeared on six different occasions to three children. Probably no other vision of the Virgin Mary has received as much publicity as those that occurred in the bleak hills of Fatima in Portugal. The first vision occurred on May 13, 1917. The children who saw it were Lucy dos Santos, 10, and her cousins Francisco, 9, and Jacinta, 7. They were tending sheep on property belonging to Lucy's father. They had just finished their rosary and were strolling a high plateau known as the Cova da Iria (Irene's Cove) when they were startled by two flashes of lightning.

The children looked skyward. It was noon and the sun was bright. Where had the lightning come from? They were truly mystified, and more so when their gaze was directed to some foliage near a small oak tree. Here they saw a globe of light, at first intensely bright and then softening into an aura which surrounded the figure of a lovely young woman.

The children were awestruck, unable to move. The lady told them not to be afraid, that she would not hurt them. Her instruction to them was to return to this exact spot on the 13th of every month until October. She said she would then identify herself. Before she faded from view she told the children to say their rosary, do penance and keep the secret.

Naturally, the children did not keep the secret despite Lucy's urgings. Francisco and Jacinta told their parents and were severely beaten for lying. Lucy was unable to contain herself. She told her parents, too, and was punished.

It was understandable that the adults were testy. Portugal, also known as the Land of Mary because of its devotion to the Immaculate Heart of Mary, was in the throes of an extremely trying period. A revolutionary republican government had overthrown the monarchy and now boasted that within two generations Catholicism in Portugal would be wiped out. The government had already abolished the Catholic sacraments. No one knew what would come next, so they were in no mood to listen to the fantasies of children.

THE SECOND VISION

It was June 13, 1917 and the three children had had plenty of time to spread the word about the Holy Mother's visit. At noon, Lucy, Francisco and Jacinta were not alone at Cova da Iria. Fifty to sixty curious villagers had followed them.

Lucy recited her rosary and then exclaimed, "I see the lightning! She is coming!"

Of course, the villagers saw nothing, but they were duly impressed by the ecstatic expressions on the children's faces. The lady's visit was a short one. The only information she imparted this time was that she would soon call Francisco and Jacinta, and Lucy would be permitted to remain on earth to spread the word of the Immaculate Heart of Mary.

She was gone. The villagers had seen nothing. Nevertheless, they were convinced that the children were not faking. They had

seen something. They were not play-acting.

The word spread incredibly fast. The village of Fatima held only a few hundred inhabitants, but when July 13th came there were more than 5,000 people on the plateau of Cova da Iria. Again, at noon, Lucy, Francisco and Jacinta stood spellbound before the small oak tree. Lucy was the spokesperson, repeating what Mary told her. She said that World War I would end soon, but that if the people did not stop offending God there would be another, more terrible war. The vision of Mary then faded.

Unfortunately for the three children, the Government came down hard on them. Before the next scheduled vision, August 13th, they were thrown in jail. The hostile government had already broken with Rome and it was determined not to permit the three children to stir up the population.

Officials tried every trick they knew to get Lucy, and Francisco to retract. They even brought the children to a cauldron of boiling oil and threatened to submerge them. Still, the little ones insisted they had seen a vision.

On August 8th, fifteen thousand people gathered at the Cova da Iria. They hoped to see a sign, but they were disappointed. The people were also outraged that the three children were in jail, so much so that Government officials decided that it would be best to release their little charges. And days later, Lucy, Jacinta and Francisco visited the Cova and saw the vision.

By this time, all of Portugal was bubbling over with excitement. Officials were worried. There was nothing they could do to stop it. Their attempts to crush Christianity in Portugal were being thwarted by three little children who knew absolutely nothing about politics or even religion, for that matter.

On September 13th more than thirty thousand people made their way to the Cova and assembled at the small oak tree. They scanned the skies. Many reported seeing a glowing globe moving from east to west. Some saw a white cloud and felt rain coming down

from a clear sky. The multitude fell on its knees when Lucy cried out that the lady was here. Tears streamed from thousands of faces. People prayed aloud. At last the Queen of Heaven had come to protect them from a hostile government.

Customarily, the Catholic Church maintains a reserved posture on the subject of miracles. But this time the Church of Lisbon asked Dr. Manuel Numes Formigao, a respected dignitary, to investigate the story. He talked to the three shepherd children and was immediately struck by the similarities reported by two children in La Salette, France. They, too, had seen Our Lady, who made the same predictions about great calamities if the French people did not stop offending God. And the doctor was unable to find any contradictions in the story put forth by Lucy, Jacinta and Francisco.

THE FINAL VISION

Lucy told Dr. Formigao that Our Lady promised a miracle during her final visit. That news spread quickly, and on October 13th the roads to Fatima were clogged with people from all walks of life—farmers, factory workers, the rich and poor, the healthy and lame. Many traveled all night to be at the Cova by noon.

Reporters from all of Portugal's leading newspapers were there to record the miracle. It rained heavily and as the hour of noon approached there was a sea of umbrellas on the high plateau. Reporters estimated that some seventy thousand people had made the pilgrimage to the Cova. Lucy was there with her little cousins, of course, and it was Lucy who cried out to the crowd. "Put away your umbrellas!"

The people were reluctant to do so because of the heavy rain, but they did do as they were told. Then Lucy shouted, "Kneel everybody! She is coming!" The rain stopped suddenly. The clouds seemed to evaporate and reveal a white hot sun shimmering in a blue sky. All 70,000 looked up in amazement.

THE MIRACLE OF THE SUN

The sun appeared to spin in the sky, shooting off fingers of

light which reached from horizon to horizon. Everyone watched in awe. This phenomenon was repeated three times. Then, suddenly, the glowing globe began to plunge toward earth. It came nearer and nearer. Women screamed that the end of the world was coming. People fell to the ground, terror-stricken. Some prayed to God to be spared. Others stood speechless as the great fiery orb plunged closer and closer.

The terror lasted for a full ten minutes. Finally, the sun halted its plunge and returned to its normal position in the sky.

Our lady had promised a miracle and had delivered it.

This heavenly display elevated the three children to almost God-like status. Everything they said was written down. Their every movement was recorded. Jacinta began having prophetic visions. Although untroubled by the knowledge that she was going to die soon, she predicted the terrible bombings of World War Two.

She saw France and Germany in ruins, and London and Frankfurt horribly damaged by bombs.

And as Our Lady predicted, Jacinta and Francisco went to Her in death. Francisco was only 11 in January, 1919 when he succumbed to influenza. Jacinta became ill. The diagnosis was that she needed a difficult chest operation. On her death bed she still had prophetic visions. When a nun told Jacinta about a wonderful sermon given by a certain priest, the little girl said, "The padre is wicked. You will see." Only a few months later the priest was forced to leave the order under a cloud.

At another time a doctor asked Jacinta to pray for him. She told him flatly, "You and your daughter will be in Heaven before me." She was right. The doctor and his daughter were dead before Jacinta passed away. Death came on February 20, 1920.

THE MIRACLES OF LUCY

Lucy reported to all who listened that Mary had told her that she was not to die soon, that Lucy was to be used to establish in the

world the devotion to Her Immaculate Heart.

The miracle of the six visions of Mary at Fatima had produced still another miracle. The incidents at Fatima had started a counter-revolution in Portugal. The vigor of the Church was restored. Portugal had returned to the Christian fold and it had been accomplished without the shedding of a single drop of blood. Many regarded that as the greatest miracle of all.

In 1925 Lucy entered the convent of the Sisters of St. Dorothy in Tuy, Spain. In December of that year she had another vision, this time of the Blessed Mother and the Christ Child. The Mother said to her:

"My child, behold my heart surrounded with the thorns that ungrateful men place therein at every moment by their blasphemies and ingratitude. You at least try to console me."

Soon, Sister Lucy began to ask for devotions to Our Lady's Immaculate Heart. She did so in 1926, 1927, and in 1929. In 1940 she sent a letter to Pius XII. In 1927 she had two visions of Christ, in which He confirmed His Mother's request for devotions. During one of the six visions of Mary at the Cova da Iria, Our Lady told the three children that before the next horrible war there would be a warning light in the sky. That light appeared in the sky over most of Western Europe on January 25, 1938. The entire sky was lighted in a crimson glow. A newspaper stated: "Aurora Borealis Startles Europe; People Flee in Fear." Experts, however, insisted that the strange light was in no way like the Aurora Borealis.

Lucy continued to work tirelessly in Our Lady's name. Finally, Pope Pius XII consecrated the Church to the Immaculate Heart of Mary on October 21, 1942. Oddly enough, Pius XII was consecrated a bishop in Rome at the very hour of the first vision of Mary at the Cova —May 13, 1917.

THE FATIMA CLUB

Monsignor Josephy Cacella of the Bronx, New York, is founder of the Fatima Club. He has had extraordinary success with the wa-

ters taken from a spring at the shrine of Fatima.

Many patients suffering from slight ailments to acute mental depression are cured after receiving a few drops of water.

The Monsignor is quick to point out that the water itself has no magical properties, but that its use presupposes purity of soul, a lively spirit of faith, and an abiding confidence.

Sister Mary Leonard of Fort Edward revealed that a patient was admitted to the hospital in Watertown, New York. He suffered severe convulsions. Specialists discovered that he had an irritation on the brain and on the lung. The patient was given some water. The lung infection cleared up completely. The irritation of the brain was reduced to such a degree that the man was able to leave the hospital and return to work. The convulsions were completely eliminated.

THE VISION ON 7th STREET

Time and again the indication is that the Virgin Mary prefers her audiences to be made up of children, at least at the outset of her miraculous appearances. On February 12, 1981, seven children were chatting on 7th Street, Hill Brothers, at Rio Piedra, Puerto Rico.

The time was about 8:30 P.M. The absolute last thing in their thoughts was the prospect of seeing a vision.

Cristina Flamer, 12, heard a soft voice say to her, "Look at me, my daughter. Look at me." She turned to find the voice and saw a figure of a woman standing under a mango tree. The woman took on the appearance of a nun, yet in seconds a change had occurred, so that now she looked like the Virgin Mary.

The other children saw the apparition, too. Cristina promptly knelt down. One child had an attack of nerves. The others stood in wide-eyed wonder. All of the children watched as the Virgin Mary spread her arms as if to embrace them, then rise off the ground, apparently levitating at will.

The children weren't the only ones who saw the Virgin. An elderly woman saw her and promptly assumed that the world was

coming to an end, or that the Son of God was going to come. Rafael Betancourt, a transporter of heavy equipment, was also a witness. He told police that the vision stayed in place throughout the night and faded away toward dawn.

When word spread through the district, parish priests talked to the young witnesses. So did police officers. As days passed and the news made its way around the world, priests and nuns from the United States sped to the area to talk to the children. Their aim was to find out if the young ones were telling the truth.

By the time the clerics from America arrived, 7th Street was jammed with curiosity-seekers and the truly religious who hoped to see the Holy Mother. One estimate had it that 10,000 people had gathered on the street, facing the mango tree.

One American priest went to Cristina Flamer's house to talk to the girl in the presence of her mother. He held up a Crucifix and said to the girl: "Do you swear upon the cross of Our Savior Jesus Christ that you have seen the Virgin? Are you sure? You know God could punish you if you lie."

Cristina kissed the cross and said, "I am telling the truth. I swear it."

Lucy Garcia, the mother of one of the young witnessess, said: "Around here there are many who are incredulous, but we remain calm in the knowledge that we have told the truth. I have seen the Virgin again tonight at about 8:30 P.M.., but if you go to that spot right now and look in that direction, you would see a pretty large cross."

Other women confirmed Lucy Garcia's statement.

Further investigation of the apparition revealed a piece of information which was quite alarming. Three of the children who had been with Cristina Flamer on the night the Virgin first appeared were Connie, Cristina and Jeannette Gonzalez. Naturally, when they went home that night they told their mother about the wondrous thing they

saw.

Mrs. Gonzalez had no reason to doubt them. She remained calm, as true Christians always do at such times, but her thoughts were with her ill mother. A few nights later as Mrs. Gonzalez was preparing for bed she heard a soft sweet voice say to her, "You should pray for your dear mother who is ill."

Mrs. Gonzalez admitted later that it was a tremendous shock to her to hear a voice tell her something like that. She knew it had to be the Virgin. The next morning she rushed to the Industrial Hospital where her mother was gravely ill. But when she arrived she was surprised to find her very much improved.

Police from Monte Hatillo questioned a great many witnesses and claimed that many of them reported that the vision sometimes faces the crowd as though to embrace it. At other times it will turn its back or hide behind the branches of the mango tree.

MARY FAVORS CHILDREN

Apparently, the Holy Mother is never concerned with the faith of her audience as long as it is young. A four-year-old boy was alone in a field one day when he looked up into the sky and saw the clouds suddenly part. A woman appeared and slowly came down to earth and stood near him. He remembered her as being stunningly attractive and radiating love. She spoke to him, but because of the passage of time he is unable to remember what she said.

Today he is an established Hollywood film director and prefers that we don't use his name. He is Jewish. But every day of his life since he was four years old he wears a necklace with the Virgin Mary around his neck.

MARY APPEARS IN RUSSIA

When Sister Lucy was involved in the six visits from the Virgin Mary in Portugal, it was said that the Holy Mother was quite concerned about Russia. Allegedly, she feared that Russia's ungodliness would do great harm to the world. Be that as it may, Mary has ap-

peared in that country's cities from time to time. Reports out of Rostov, Kharkhov, and Leningrad confirm it. Such visits always renew religious fervor, which is looked upon disfavorably by the Russian hierarchy.

Nevertheless, the Virgin does appear. The first apparition is thought to have occurred on July 13, 1962 in the Janovai Collectivised Zone in Skiamonial, in Lithunia, a republic of the U.S.S.R.

And again it was a child who had the privilege of seeing Mary—18-year-old Franzeska Remova Macugs. The girl suddenly found herself surround by a strange light. In front of her she saw a white altar on which there were six burning candles. Then the Blessed Virgin appeared, dressed in white with a blue sash around her waist. Her face appeared to be in pain, as though she was suffering. (Incredibly, Sister Lucy noted, too, that talk of Russia appeared to cause suffering in Mary's face).

Now, Franzeska watched as Mary raised her arms and then faded from view. The apparition said nothing to her. However, the Holy Mother appeared to the girl again on another occasion. This time the vision stood on a white cloth dotted with small red crosses. And she spoke to the girl, saying:

"You have been chosen because of your simplicity. I cannot save men from destruction if they will not return to God." Her face again appeared to be suffering.

Devotees constructed an altar of white stones on the exact spot where the Blessed Virgin stood. Again and again the Communist Youth Movement has destroyed the altar, but it is always reconstructed.

It was reported that the holy in Russia have said: "The Mother of God is appearing in various parts of our fatherland in order to open our eyes. She wants us to pray more fervently so that the world may be saved from destruction."

It is not easy to pick up stories out of the Soviet Union. Usually, they are quashed instantly. However, a recent vision did get by

the censors, and we now know that Mary appeared in a village called Tombow, 25 miles from Moscow. The feeling was that Mary would eventually appear in the capital.

At the Tombow sighting, Mary manifested herself in the form of a white hand in a clear sky. It held a huge pen and wrote the following words:

"There is still more evil than good in the world! It is winter for my people. Now is the time of repentance. No good soul will be left among the evil ones; and no evil soul will be left among the good ones. Heed my warning. Produce fruits or repentance. I will save the God-fearing. Accept your responsibilities. The time is very near at hand. I will return soon.

"Amen."

According to witnesses, the white hand continued to write across the sky for thirty minutes. The writing held in place for more than two hours and was seen everywhere in the city. In fact, many of the people who saw it were frightened. Leaders who saw what was happening were unable to do anything about it. They watched helplessly as traffic was tied up and thousands of pedestrians stared at the sky.

SUN HALO PRECEDES VISION

Early in 1981, over the south coast of Puerto Rico, at about noon, a brilliant, multicolored circle, or halo, appeared around the sun. The phenomenon lasted for about two hours, which was long enough for thousands of people to be aware of it. The unusual sight was especially prominent in Ponce and its environs. Radio stations and newspaper offices received hundreds of calls. Police Chief in Coano, told reporters: "The sun was orange, red, blue ...around that circle was a golden border. It was beautiful. It was difficult to stop looking at it."

Soon after that uncanny manifestation in the sky, the Virgin Mary made her appearance in Puerto Rico. Was there a link? We can only speculate. It does, however, appear that the Holy Mother

may have been trying to prepare the people of Puerto Rico for her visit.

And there does seem to be a correlation between Mary and the sun. Remember, there were 70,000 people in Portugal who witnessed the miracle of the sun during Mary's appearance.

VISION OF CHRIST'S FACE

It was the Wednesday after Easter, 1977. The locale was the Holy Trinity Episcopal Church in Shamokin, Pennsylvania. About 25 worshippers were praying when a little girl cried, "Look, grandma, on the cloth—It's God's face!" The cloth she referred to was the white brocade cloth covering the altar tabernacle where consecrated bread is kept. At that time the cloth had been in use for 15 years. But now, strangely, a pattern of shadows on it blended to resemble the face of Jesus Christ. All 25 parishioners stared at the face in disbelief. One housewife said later,

"We called our friends and told them they had to come to the church immediately. We were afraid it would go away." It did not go away. During the next few weeks the story of the Christ of the tabernacle cloth spread all over the United States.

Busloads of people arrived in Shamokin from as far away as California and Texas. The small, coal-mining town of 12,000 was hardly equipped to house their visitors.

On one occasion a band of gypsies pulled up in front of the church in a red Rolls-Royce. They crawled on their hands and knees to the altar to gaze at the cloth. They deposited 13 dozen red roses at the altar before they left.

By the end of May, more than 60,000 people had visited the small church. On weekends there were lines of curious people stretching for blocks. For those who had come in search of healing powers, five priests were on duty at all times to anoint them. There were lay readers who prayed every thirty minutes for the thousands who were too sick to make the journey. Four of the pilgrims who visited the shrine claimed that their severe sicknesses had been

cured.

The miracle cloth was moved, occasionally, but movement did not disturb the face. What's more, not all saw the face. Some said they saw two kneeling figures, or Jesus standing with a staff, or the Virgin Mary. In any case, something was there to see. One reporter said that she observed "a vague impression of two eyes, a jaw line, a nose and possibly hair. It's perfectly visible, just as you spot a horse in a cloud after someone has suggested that it is there."

Parish Priest Frank R. Knutti, 70, had the good sense to keep the phenomenon from becoming a sideshow. He banned all concession stands and bumper stickers. He said: "Whatever it is, it's good and people have gotten a tremendous uplift from it. I want to share it but I don't want it to become a sideshow."

Bishop Dean Stevenson of Harrisburg was an early visitor to the church. He said he was "aware of a presence which strengthened me. We don't have a lot of experience with such things, and there is no procedure in the diocese for it. I have no idea where this might lead."

Oddly enough, it was again a child who first saw the apparition on the cloth.

MARY vs. COMMUNISTS

The Holy Mother is perhaps the only entity who has been able to outwit the Soviets on a regular basis. Her appearances behind the Iron Curtain has always stymied the Communists. As atheists, they cannot accept her presence, nor can they control the people fortunate enough to witness her manifestations.

The KGB usually refers to the visions as being perpetrated by the CIA, with trick cameras. That is, if the news of a vision leaks out to the free world. If it doesn't, then the Soviets need only deal with its own people, those who have witnessed the apparition. What they do is insist to the thousands of such witnesses that they have been the subjects of mass hypnosis, or will offer some other lame reason for the vision. They also suggest that if the "enemy" is captured she

will be placed in a concentration camp or a mental hospital.

We don't know how often the Blessed Virgin has appeared to the Russians. Despite the Communist regime, Russia is a holy nation. Christians and Jews do pray in secret. It makes sense that Mary would appear to them sooner than she would to those who don't suffer religious repression. Remember, Portugal was on the verge of becoming a godless nation when Mary appeared to Sister Lucy and her cousins.

There are reports that the Holy Mother is now frustrating Fidel Castro in Cuba. The country is another which is extremely religious. It's understandable that Mary would come to those people to bolster their faith in Christianity. According to widespread belief, Mary appears shortly before a terrible disaster strikes the island or just prior to a bloodbath caused by war or revolution. No wonder Castro is troubled by such apparitions.

THE MIRACLE PAINTING

The year was 1531. A Christian Aztec Indian named Juan Diego saw a vision of the Holy Mother. According to legend, the Virgin asked Juan to go to the bishop of Mexico and request that a shrine be built in her honor.

Juan did as he was told, but was flatly turned down by the bishop. Later, the Virgin again appeared to the Indian, only this time she gave him some fresh flowers and told him to deliver them to the unbelieving churchman.

Juan wrapped the flowers in his tilma, which is a poncho-like garment made of cactus fibers. He gave the cloak to the bishop.

When the padre opened the tilma he received a terrible shock. The flowers were gone. Not even a petal remained. And in their place was a painting of the Holy Mother on the rough cloth!

We have come to know this work as the Virgin of Guadalupe, and it can be seen at the Basilica of Our Lady of Guadalupe. In fact, millions of pilgrims have seen it since 1531, and thousands have

claimed that they were cured of crippling diseases after viewing Mary's face on the cloth.

Is the story fact or fantasy? The Catholic Church has always maintained that the painting was created by a miracle. But she has had no evidence to back up the statement until recently, when Dr. Philip Callahan, an expert in infrared photography at the University of Florida in Gainseville, was asked to examine the work.

That request was made by Jody Smith, a philosopher at Pensacola State College. Both journeyed to Mexico City and used scientific methods to test the painting. The methods were similar to those used to test the Holy Shroud of Turin.

The scientists' conclusion was that the Virgin of Guadalupes' work had been done by a divine hand!

Dr. Callahan used highly sophisticated equipment to study the more than 40 photographs he took of the painting. He said later, "Infrared waves will go through a lot of paint. It will reveal images not ordinarily visible. If you can see a drawing underneath the visible layer, you know it's not miraculous.

"It's not like any other painting that exists," Dr. Callahan continued. "I could not find any semblance of brush strokes or spatula strokes under it. It's not done in oils; it's not done in water colors. I don't know what it is!

"The first thing we discovered was that a lot of additions had been made to the original picture of the Virgin. The decorative additions are all chipping and fading. But the original underneath looks like it was painted yesterday.

"And another mystery is the cactus cloth it's painted on. It's a very simple cloth and should have rotted away within 30 years—50 at most. Yet the painted cloth has been in an open basilica for centuries. There doesn't seem to be any way to explain it. I think it's miraculous!"

THE HOLY SHROUD OF TURIN

A great many mysteries surround the cloth that Christ was supposedly buried in at approximately 30 A.D. One of the most puzzling aspects of the Shroud is its disappearance for 1,300 years. It wasn't discovered until the 1350s in Lirey, France.

One theory has it that after the Shroud was removed from the empty tomb it was folded so that only Christ's face was visible. It was then taken to Edessa, Turkey, where it remained until 57 A.D. One historian believes that when a Turkish king decided to persecute Christians, the Shroud was hidden in the walls of the city's west gate to keep it from being destroyed by the king.

The shroud was not rediscovered until 525 when a flood destroyed most of Edessa. It was then venerated as the Madylion, a classic description of Christ's face. Edessa was besieged by the Byzantines in 943. The Shroud was seized and taken to Constantinople, now known as Istanbul. The sacred cloth vanished again in 1204 when that city was sacked. The theory here is that it was stolen by a crusader named Geoffrey de Charnay.

When the Holy Shroud reappeared in 1350, it was bought by the Duke of Savoy and placed on display. Two centuries later, 1532, the church in which the Shroud was kept caught fire. It was a miracle that the cloth survived. The damage was minimal—a few scorch marks from drops of molten silver from the casket which housed the cloth. In 1578, the heirs of the Duke of Savoy moved the Shroud to its present location in Turin.

WHAT SCIENTISTS LEARNED ABOUT THE SHROUD

As you undoubtedly know, scientists examined and tested the 14 foot by 14 foot linen cloth for three years. The tests were rigorous.

The scientific team was international and used the most sophisticated space-age techniques available.

They have proved that a long-held theory that the Shroud was the work of a 14th Century artist was wrong. Samuel Pellicori, an optical physicist at the Santa Barbara Research Center, conducted extensive chemical tests, and concluded: 'There is absolutely no trace of paint on the Shroud.'

Church officials permitted the scientists to enter the Cathedral of St. John the Baptist in Turin, where the Shroud is housed, to conduct their tests. The only experiment the church has frowned on is the Carbon-14 test, which would reveal the Shroud's age. This is understandable. To conduct the Carbon-14 test, a very large portion of the Shroud would have to cut away.

Tests, however, do prove that the stains on the cloth were made by blood and not paint or dye. Scientists have also determined that the male figure was 5 feet $10^1/_2$ inches tall and weighed 175 pounds, and was about 30 years old. The face was unmistakably Jewish in appearance.

It was shown, too, that the face had been severely beaten, with a possible broken nose and badly swollen eyes. There were numerous cuts and bruises on his cheeks.

Scientists have also just about settled the age-old question which asks: Who crucified Jesus; the Jews or the Romans? The lash wounds on the back indicate that Jesus took between 90 and 120 lashes. Hebrew law at that time specified that no one was to receive more than 39 lashes. The Romans had no such limit. The wounds are of the type that would have been inflicted by the Roman flagra, or whips with two or three metal-tipped thongs.

Scientists discovered from the Shroud that Christ was nailed to the cross through his wrists, not his hands. This accounts for the lack of thumbs on the man on the Shroud. A nail driven through the wrist at a certain angle will touch the median nerve and cause the thumb to contract into the palm. The Shroud revealed to the scien-

tists that the man had carried a heavy object on his back. His shoulders had been rubbed raw and one of them may have been dislocated.

A headpiece had been placed on the man's crown and had caused numerous gashes. The scalp had been punctured. The "cap" may have been made up of sharp thorns.

Tests showed that the man had bruised knees and that they were dirty from repeated falls. The man on the Shroud wore his hair in the style of Biblical times; in a ponytail,

It was shown that the man suffered a two-inch wound between the fifth and sixth ribs on the right side, possibly made by a spear.

Coins were placed over his eyes after death. The people of the day felt that the spirit would be locked into the body if coins were so placed. The coins here were identified as Judean, issued during the reign of Pontius Pilate.

SPIRITUAL AWAKENING OF THE SCIENTISTS

Many of the learned men who conducted the tests on the Holy Shroud of Turin were atheists or agnostics. Before the tests were only partially completed, many of these men experienced an amazing spiritual awakening.

Some of the researchers admitted that their experiences in Turin were unique and powerful, that their lives were changed both professionally and personally.

Still another revelation came from Donald Lynn, deputy manager of the flight science office on the Voyager project, who worked on the Shroud. He says, "Money has appeared just when we needed it, and equipment has worked when the odds were against it. Too many things happened that had no business happening. The hand of God has been very evident in all the things I have done relating to the Shroud."

As we said earlier, the only test not yet conducted by scientists is the Carbon 14 dating test. This is not likely to take place, ac-

cording to Vatican sources, because it would involve burning part of the Shroud. The dating process measures the amount of radioactive carbon an item gives off when burned, and thereby determines the age of the item.

But then, what more proof do we need that the Shroud of Turin was once wrapped around the body of Christ?

ANSWERED PRAYERS

Psychiatrist Dr. Robert Laidlaw once wrote: "We should remember the words of Steinmetz, the electrical genius of the General Electric Company, who stated that the next realm for research was the spiritual, and the next field that of prayer."

Dr. Smiley Blanton, another psychiatrist, reported his conversation with the minister, Dr. Norman Vincent Peale. Dr. Blanton told him: "Prayer is the greatest power in the world. It is a pity that more people do not know how to use it."

Dr. Blanton added: "I have been praying for years that some of you gentlemen of the clergy would stop being suspicious of us psychiatrists, would see that in our separate ways we're working for the same goal; the salvation of human souls. Looks to me as if you might be the answer to that prayer. I've always thought we could make more progress working together than either religion or psychiatry could make working alone."

Dr. Peale agreed. The two worked out a general plan by which Dr. Blanton would take Dr. Peale's more difficult cases and attempt to analyze them from a psychiatric view.

Dr. Blanton said: "Neither of us foresaw, even dimly, what lay ahead. So great was the demand for this dual approach to human problems that almost immediately we found ourselves swamped. We organized a clinic at Marble Church, and called it, for lack of a more descriptive term, The Psychiatric Clinic. As time went on, we brought in more pastors, more psychiatrists, more psychologists. Still, we could not keep up with the requests for aid.

"In 1951 the clinic was incorporated as the American Foundation of Religion and Psychiatry. Last year our staff of thirty-five ex-

perts gave over six thousand hours of individual counseling. In addition we conduct a psychiatric training program to help clergymen, chaplains and social workers of all faiths. We have set up a research program that includes the study of religious healing, the mysterious area where the faith of the individual seems to reach out and touch the healing power of God. We are trying to encourage other groups throughout the nation to set up similar clinics. If we succeed I firmly believe that we shall reverse the trend that has made mental illness our most critical national health problem and keeps more than half of our hospital beds full of confused and despairing people."

The power of prayer is finally becoming recognized as a force to be reckoned with. Other prayer movements have been started throughout the United States with great success. The North Carolina Baptist Hospital in Salem has combined the talents of a doctor, psychiatrist and a minister to restore patients to health. The minister of this healing team, Reverend Richard K. Young, says hospitals can be great centers for prayer, adding that the legend over the door of New York City's Columbia-Presbyterian Hospital reads: "For of the Most High cometh healing."

PROOF THAT PRAYER WORKS

It is not easy to find proof that everyone can accept, but Franklin Loehr did it. He was a chemist as well as theologian, and with the help of 150 people he conducted experiments that proved beyond a doubt that God does answer prayers.

At the Religious Research Foundation, Reverend Loehr conducted a series of experiments of prayer on plants. There were more than 700 experiments, using 27,000 seeds and seedlings. Over 100,000 measurements were taken. These experiments were supplemented and corroborated by six other experimental groups.

Some of the people who participated in the experiments were well-known in their fields. There were Dr. Sorokin of Harvard, Aldous Huxley, Bishop Gerald Heard, and Dr. Norman Vincent Peale.

The assistants were divided into two groups. One group was

instructed to pray for the well-being of the seeds, and to pray that God would reveal Himself through them and through the plants that grew out of them. The other groups were given soil and seeds for planting, but were instructed not to pray.

Incredibly, the seeds that were prayed over grew three to four times faster than those without prayer. Some individuals got better results than others, but all were effective.

Dr. Loehr drew the following conclusions from his work:

1. Those who used strong thoughts (prayer) got results.

2. Green-thumb gardeners got their results by love. "I told them (the seeds) that I loved them and how happy I was with them," was one technique, repeated in many cases, which led to the basic discovery of the emotional power of prayer. Those who prayed with feeling surpassed those who used thought.

3. The best results were obtained by those persons who prayed to God, without adding their own feeling or thought, but asking only for spiritual aid.

4. Prayer is only one factor. Sometimes additional attitudes helped speed results. For instance, "The Lord helps those who help themselves." In some instances, faith itself helped. Skepticism acted as a retardant. It was thought that skepticism brought with it a lack of confidence, and that it divided one's mental powers. It was learned that clarity helped. And if members on a prayer team disagreed, the prayer work suffered.

Dr. Loehr said, "Prayer is such a vast power that our research has only scratched the surface." The well-known prayer healer Agnes Sanford has achieved phenomenal success through prayer. She says she begins by asking for spiritual help. She indicates that a vacuum cleaner won't work until it is plugged into an electrical outlet, saying that spiritual power is akin to electricity and that we are merely the channel through which it may operate.

HOW TO ORGANIZE YOUR PRAYER

Relax.

Accept or "turn on" the power, which may be had for the asking.

Direct that power to what you want accomplished.

Visualize it as you want it to be.

Give thanks that it is being accomplished.

If you are unaware of the best solution to a problem, and you find it difficult or impossible to visualize the outcome, simply pray for the best solution. Assume the attitude of "Not my will, but Thine be done."

A PRAYER SUGGESTION

One prayer that has for ages brought people universal light is the one favored by Saint Francis of Assisi:

"Lord, make me the instrument of your peace. Where there is hatred, let me sow love. Where there is injury, pardon. Where there is doubt, faith. Where there is despair, hope. Where there is darkness, light; and where there is sadness, joy.

"O Divine Master, grant that I may not so much seek to be consoled, as to console, to be understood, as to understand; to be loved as to love. For it is in giving that we receive. It is in pardoning that we are pardoned. And it is in dying that we are born to eternal life."

THE BRANDEN REPORT

A report by the National Council of Churches on faith healing in American Protestantism indicated that many reputable ordained ministers regularly practice some form of faith healing.

The report was prepared by Dr. Charles A. Branden, a professor of Religion and Literature of Religions at Northwestern University. More than thirty percent of the ministers who replied to his

questionnaire said that they had healed sixty-four different diseases through prayer.

An officer of the National Council of Churches said, "The Branden Report was only a survey. There was no obligation for ministers to submit detailed medical reports. Nevertheless, the respondents were very conservative in their claims."

"In almost every case," said Dr. Branden, "the informant declared that the diagnosis had been made by a competent medical doctor. There had been medical treatment for a period of time.

"One case of cancer of the lungs," the doctor continued, "had persisted for two years and was properly diagnosed and treated by a physician. After the healing, which consisted of laying on of the hands, some ritual and prayer at a healing service, X-ray tests disclosed the condition had cleared. In a period of six months prior to the reporting of the case there had been no recurrence."

A minister from the Midwest reported curing a 37-year-old woman of lung cancer. One week before the healing she had been examined by several physicians and told that she had only a few days to live. The minister and the woman prayed together. She confessed her sins. She forgave a woman she hated. The following morning her lungs were cleared of cancer. Several years later the woman was still free of the dreaded disease.

A minister in Denver, Colorado reported that he went to see a man who had been bed-ridden for two years. He had a tubercular condition that was so serious his doctors had abandoned all hope of recovery.

The minister prayed over the man and conducted a "laying on of the hands" ritual. The cure was immediate. According to the minister, the man was back at work two days later, with no sign of the tuberculosis.

Dr. Branden said that 80 percent of the healing ministers said that their cures were permanent. Often, several years had elapsed since the healing had occurred, and there was no evidence of recur-

rence of the disease. Dr. Branden considered two years as the cut-off time. After that, the patient was considered permanently cured.

All of the ministers to a man agreed that there is no miraculous power in their hands. "It is not the minister's hands," said one, "but God who does the healing."

AGNES SANFORD'S AMAZING POWER

We mentioned Agnes Sanford earlier. She was the wife of an Episcopalian minister in Westboro, Massachusetts, and the author of a book on healing called *"The Healing Light."*

One of her most amazing feats of healing through prayer occurred when an eight-year-old girl in Asheville, North Carolina was stricken with a virus inflammation of the brain and spinal cord. She lay in a hospital, paralyzed from the waist down, with a temperature of 106 degrees.

Her father was a doctor. He and other doctors were helpless in controlling the girl's continual convulsions.

The hospital's chaplain telephoned Mrs. Sanford. A physician friend of Agnes Sanford's was in the hospital at the time. She asked to speak to him. Mrs. Sanford told the doctor that at precisely 9:30 P.M. that night he was to place his hands on the girl's body. "I'll begin my prayers at that moment," Mrs. Sanford said.

One witness in the hospital room said later: "The doctor entered the room where a nurse was using chloroform to try to anesthetize the patient so that further convulsions might be prevented. At the time, the convulsions occurred every three or four minutes. "The doctor placed his hands on the child at precisely 9:30 P.M.

He had no sooner touched the patient when a relaxed sigh rose from her lips and she fell into a deep, natural sleep. The convulsions ceased and the child seemed very relaxed.

"The following morning, the child was still sleeping. Her right side was no longer paralyzed and, by afternoon, life came back into her entire body. Ten days later, the patient was released from the

hospital and returned to her home."

Before the year was out, the girl was completely cured. Since then she grew into a healthy young woman, with no recurrence of her affliction.

THE GIRL WHO PRAYED FOR A CURE

Her name was Pauline Scott. She was nine years old when she was diagnosed as having an incurable blood disease. The girl's relatives were told by a doctor that there was no hope for her. He even suggested that they take her to a religious healing shrine and pray for a miracle.

Before the relatives could get her to a shrine, Pauline's condition worsened. She was placed in an oxygen tent. One doctor said, "She has only a few days to live."

Pauline said later: "I heard a doctor and a nurse talking near my bed. They thought I was asleep and they said it would be doubtful if I lived until morning.

"I prayed to get well. I was all alone and as I prayed I felt that God was listening. Don't ask me how I felt it, I just did. I prayed very hard. Then something happened. The disease disappeared. I think it was a miracle that did it."

"The Family Doctor," a medical magazine in England, said that Pauline's case was an outstanding example of miraculous healing.

ARTHUR FORD SPEAKS

Arthur Ford, America's most famous medium, said this of prayer:

"Even though we know that God knows our problems, including the way we came to be tangled into them, still we usually feel that we have specifically to get them out before him. Some people talk them out just as they would to a friend. They may speak aloud or they may whisper as if the least expression were enough for his ear.

Some explain their dilemma mentally. However the problem is presented, the prayer is the same—"God help me!"

"This call for help is the key to answered prayer because we would not be holding up our problem to God, and ourself with it, unless we had some belief that He could help us. The strength of our belief is the measure of the answer we will receive. According to our faith, so shall it be! This is the fundamental law of prayer. Everyone who has spoken with authority on prayer has told us this thing. It was the keynote of the teaching of Jesus. Believe that you have it, and you have it. Faith is the activating agent. The answer to our need is available but it cannot get into us until we call for it and believe it will come. I wish I knew how to make this point clear for it is paramount."

-*Nothing So Strange*, by Arthur Ford

STIGMATA

Stigmata refers to the spontaneously formed wounds which correspond to those suffered by Christ when He was crucified. There were five wounds. One in each hand, one in each foot, and the spear wound in the side. Some stigmatics have also suffered the seven wounds caused by the crown of thorns on Jesus' head. Stigmata have appeared on the bodies of more than 330 people since the time of St. Francis of Assisi. Roman Catholic Church authorities are slow to recognize stigmata as miraculous. Their feeling in most cases is that stigmata is the result of conscious or unconscious suggestion. Most stigmatics were priests, nuns or monks who admitted to being prone to brooding over the Crucifixion. Nevertheless, there is no explanation for the real wounds they suffered, except that they were miracles.

ST. FRANCIS OF ASSISI

History tells us that St. Francis, an Italian saint born in 1182 and died in 1226, was the first known individual who showed evidence of stigmata.

Francis was born into a wealthy merchant family but was something of a delinquent during his teen years. He then converted into a pious life and adopted the vows of poverty. He imitated Jesus Christ rather assiduously throughout his life and became famous for his love of all animals.

Two years before his death he was on Mount Alverno in the Apennines when he saw a vision. What he saw was a fiery angel with six wings carrying a crucified man.

At this point Francis went into a sort of ecstatic trance, and when he regained consciousness he saw that his hands and feet were bleeding, as though they had been pierced by long nails. There was

also a spear wound in his side.

The wounds were attested to by two popes, Gregory IX and Alexander IV.

ST. CATHERINE OF SIENA

Catherine was an Italian nun and a visionary who lived from 1347 to 1380, just 33 years, which was the exact number of years Jesus was on earth.

At the age of 19, Catherine was a volunteer nurse, but she was a go-getter. She had plenty of charisma and drive. If Catherine were alive today she would undoubtedly be in the forefront of the ERA movement. In fact, she eventually came to wield great power in the church and the state.

Apparently, Catherine was a workaholic. She rarely rested. Two hours of sleep a night was plenty for the lady, and she also managed to get along on a handful of herbs a day.

Catherine was a remarkable woman. She was educated at a time when very few people in the world knew how to read and write. What's more, Catherine would take great delight in writing to Kings and to the Pope, who was Gregory XI. She used to tease the Pope by calling him "Dear little Babbo."

Catherine had stigmata. She was not proud of the wounds and would keep them hidden. It is not known if she did any brooding over the Crucifixion. One would tend to think that she did not, considering her warm, outgoing personality and her constant high good humor.

When you look at statues of St. Catherine of Siena, don't bother to look for wounds. Pope Sixtus IV ordered that they never be shown on her statues.

ST. RITA OF CASCIA

Rita is an Italian saint who lived from 1381 to 1457. She is a rather sad case. You might say that she was an early victim of wife

abuse. She was only 12 years old when she was forced to marry a rich nobleman who was extremely brutal to her right from the beginning. But Rita did something about her abuse that most wives today never think of doing, nor even consider doing. Rita was patient. Through lots of affection she managed to change the roaring bull of a man into a loving mate. And after 18 years of marriage he died.

In 1452 Rita entered the Augustinian convent in Cascia. One day she listened to a missionary preach about the passions of Christ. She then prayed ardently that she too would feel those passions.

She did feel the sharp thorns that punctured Christ's forehead. And wounds did appear elsewhere on her body. Skeptics of the day called those wounds the result of smallpox. In any event, the open sores did become wormy and fetid. Rita was isolated as a leper. Legend has it that on the day she died, holy rays emanated from her puncture wounds.

ST. VERONICA GIULIANI

Veronica was an Italian nun who lived from 1660 to 1697. She was 33 when she saw a vision of Christ nailed to the cross. It was Good Friday. Veronica developed stigmata during the vision when it was said that rays went from Christ's wounds to her hands, feet and side.

The wounds healed, then opened again until she died. The spear wound in her side, however, never healed. It bled constantly. For disbelievers, Veronica drew a picture of the heart wounds she suffered. After her death, her heart was removed. The scars on the heart matched exactly the picture Veronica had drawn.

ANNA KATHARINA EMMERICH

Anna was a German nun who lived from 1774 to 1824. There was nothing special about Anna. She was born to a peasant family who gave her a job of being the cow keeper on the farm. Anna was a sickly girl. She entered the convent at Agnetenberg in 1803, but it did nothing for her ailments. But even though she was sickly, she

spent her nights making clothes for the poor. At the age of 37, she developed stigmata. She had wounds on her hands and feet, a spear wound in her side, thorn wounds on her head and a double cross on her breast.

The nuns in her convent prayed that her wounds would be healed, and they were. Still, every Friday until her death, the wounds opened and bled.

MARIA VON MORL

Little is known about Maria. She lived from 1812 to 1868. She had stigmata on her hands, feet and side. Her distinction is that the wounds were seen by more than 40,000 people.

LOUISE LATEAU

Louise was a French seamstress who lived from 1850 to 1883. She was the daughter of a working-class family. During the horrendous cholera epidemic of 1866 Louise cast aside her own fears about catching the dreaded disease and nursed those who were afflicted in her hometown of Bois d'Haine.

Then she, too, fell ill with the disease. However, Louise had a miraculous recovery which astounded everyone. In 1868 she developed stigmata. The wounds appeared only Fridays between 1:00 and 2:00 P.M., and between 4:00 and 5:00 P.M. During those periods the wounds bled, but did not bleed at any other time during the week.

ST. GEMMA GALGANI

Gemma was an Italian saint who lived from 1878 to 1903. She was not permitted to live with her parents when she was very young because there was tuberculosis in the family. She had to stay with relatives. After her father died when she was 20, Gemma had to leave her relatives' home. The girl then existed in extreme poverty.

Many considered it a miracle that she survived the frightful conditions under which she lived. Yet an even greater miracle came her way when doctors at a hospital diagnosed Gemma as having tuberculosis of the spine. After a lengthy period of earnest pray-

ing, a miracle occurred. The disease disappeared!

Gemma was the recipient of still another miracle. Not yet 21, she had a vision of St. Gabriel Possenti. That vision convinced her that she should join the Passionist convent. But Gemma was crushed when she was turned down. To keep herself alive, she found work as a housekeeper. At the age of 21, Gemma developed stigmata. She had all of the wounds— hands, feet, side and forehead and even had scourge marks on her back and shoulders. Those were the whip lashes that Christ suffered when he was forced to carry his own cross.

Gemma was extremely pious. The wounds appeared only on Fridays, but the girl prayed everyday. She prayed so often that others teased her about it.

Pope Pius XII canonized Gemma in 1940.

PADRE PIO

Padre Pio was an Italian priest, miracle worker and a clairvoyant. He lived from 1887 to 1968. Padre Pio's given name was Francesco Forgione. He was ordained a monk of the Capuchin order in 1918. He bled a teacup full of blood every day of his life until he died.

Padre Pio is not yet a saint, although he has the required three miracles for canonization. There may have been more than three miracles. But on the record is the restoring of sight to a girl who had no pupils in her eyes, raising the dead, and curing incurable cancer. One pilgrim proclaimed, "I was there when Padre Pio picked hunchbacks off the floor and straightened their backs. I saw him cure cripples."

Padre Pio's Christ-like wounds have never been officially accepted by the church. He attracted so much attention in 1923 that he was barred from saying Mass or even receiving visitors. That ban lasted until 1931.

Father John Soorento, director of the New York Archdiocese's Italian Council explained, "He was investigated by the Vatican for

the crass commerciality surrounding him."

The stigmata was quite real. Padre Pio had five open wounds that never healed. He had them for fifty years, yet in all that time they never became infected, never reddened and never became swollen. His chest wounds formed the shape of an inverted cross. When Padre Pio served Mass he always wore gloves with the fingers cut off so that his palm wounds would not show.

It was his habit to say Mass every morning at 5 A.M. in the tiny Church of San Giovanni Rotondo in the hamlet at Pietrelcina in southern Italy. Nearly every morning the church was filled with scores of Catholics, rich and poor, sick and well, hoping to see someone cured by a miracle.

The most awe-inspiring part of the Mass, however, was in witnessing Padre Pio himself. During the consecration of the wine, Padre Pio would stare into the contents of the chalice. The old priest's eyes would become glazed. And he would sometimes keep his gaze unwaveringly on the wine for upwards of two hours.

Today, the body of Padre Piorests in a crypt at Santa Maria delle Griazle in San Giovanni Rotondo

He is surrounded by flowers and trees. His followers know that someday Padre Pio will become a saint.

THERESE NEUMANN

Therese Neumann was a farm girl in Germany and she lived from 1898 to 1962. Hers is the most recent case of stigmata on record.

In 1918, when she was 20, she hurt herself fighting a fire. For a short time after that experience she was paralyzed, although doctors were unable to find anything wrong with her. Actually, her health was broken. For several years she was the victim of unexplained sicknesses. During one of these years she became blind and bedridden, but had a miraculous recovery. This seizure occurred after she was milking a cow. Therese suffered a convulsion, with blindness as the result.

Later, she began to assume other people's illnesses. In one instance she heard about a theology student who had a throat ailment which was so serious he was going to be dismissed from the seminary because of it. Therese prayed to God to cure him and let her assume the ailment instead.

Soon after her prayers she began to cough and spit up blood. An abscess formed on her throat. It was very difficult for Therese to get anything down, even water. The student no longer had a throat ailment and he eventually became a priest.

Eventually, Therese rallied, but in 1926, during the season of Lent, she became sick again. With a fever raging within her, she kept repeating the same thought: "Our Divine Saviour has suffered much more for us."

On the first Thursday night of Lent, Therese saw a vision of Jesus Christ. He was in the Garden of Olives and it was the night before the Crucifixion. He was kneeling among trees and rocks.

Therese was able to see that he was in agony. She suddenly began to share that agony. There was a sudden, deep pain in her side. Her left side felt as though it was on fire. The pain was so severe that she thought she was going to die. Therese felt the spot where it hurt and was aware of warm blood on her hand. She could feel the blood oozing down her body.

The vision faded, but the bleeding continued until noon the next day. But many visions came to her during that period of Lent. Therese saw Roman soldiers beating Jesus with whips. This was after his trial before Pilate.

She saw the soldiers making the crown of thorns and Therese saw them place it on Christ's head. She saw and heard the soldiers mocking Jesus because he claimed to be the King of the Jews.

During the fourth week of Lent, Therese walked with Jesus as he carried the cross on his back all the way from the city to the hill called Golgotha, where the Romans held their executions. Golgotha overlooked Jerusalem.

Between the hours of noon and three o'clock on Good Friday, Therese appeared to be in a trance and she also appeared to be suffering all of the agony that Christ suffered on the cross. Therese bled from her side. Her hands and feet bled. Seven ugly and bloody scars appeared on her forehead.

In 1927 Therese took no nourishment except for the Holy Communion. And on every Good Friday until her death she bled from her side, her hands and feet, and her forehead. Thousands of Roman Catholics made pilgrimages to her home to witness the stigmata. She was considered by many to be a saint.

Therese Neumann died in Konnersreuth, Germany. She was 64.

MIRACLES OF HEALING

It must be stated at the outset that the American Medical Association does not consider miracle healing as a valid course of endeavor. It stated not long ago: "The medical profession recognizes the power of faith on the individual mind as a factor that may affect the condition of sick people. There are occasional instances in which diseases generally regarded as uniformly fatal reverse themselves without any explainable medical cause, whether or not the patient has had the ministrations of so-called healers.

"If such a phenomenon were to occur to an individual under 'treatment' by one of these healers, the likelihood is that he or she would take the credit. But the medical profession does not recognize that 'faith healing' as such has any accepted merit whereby it can be regarded as having remedial or curative effect in persons who are actually victims of organic disease."

Nevertheless, in the past twenty years miracle healing has had some fantastic results. Newspapers and radio and television networks have seen fit to publish and film the wonders of miracle healing demonstrations conducted by Oral Roberts and other gifted ministers. Seminarians today are investigating the field and many priests and ministers are studying all the information on the subject they can get hold of and are actually testing their abilities with miracle healing.

THE GREEK SHEPHERD HEALER

One of the most startling cases on record of miracle healing occurred in 1941 in Athens, Greece. The healer, Athanasios Contogeorge, was a shepherd who learned early in life that he had the power to heal animals. It wasn't until he was 28 years old that he

knew he could also heal people.

Athanasios' first human patient was a boy with crooked legs. He was successful in straightening them. Word spread so quickly that Athanasios was soon seeing 60 patients a day.

Athanasios was called "Vlahos," which means shepherd in Greek. Vlahos soon became an international celebrity. He treated King Paul of Greece for a broken foot. When Haile Selassie of Ethiopia visited Greece he suffered a sciatica attack. Vlahos was called to treat him. Vlahos also treated the American and British Ambassadors.

Then one day Vlahos found himself in court. He was being sued by the medical profession for practicing medicine without a license. One doctor sneered, "He is illiterate. He has no legal certificate to practice medicine. He is a charlatan. He must be stopped."

At this point Vlahos challenged the doctors present. He said,

"If they can do what I am about to do, I will stop my healing." The judge told him to go ahead. The doctors were suspicious. They assumed Vlahos was going to do something theatrical, a trick.

The shepherd went to the rear of the courtroom where a lamb was tied. He brought the animal up front, then broke two of its legs. There was no doubt that the legs were broken. Everyone heard the snapping bones and saw the bones sticking through the skin.

Vlahos set the broken legs and stood the lamb up on its feet. The animal ran around the courtroom as though nothing had happened. The doctors examined the animal and were astonished.

Vlahos glared at the doctors and said, "Now, which of you will do the same?"

The healing shepherd won the case. He said to the judge, "The power of God goes through my hands." And no one doubted him.

MIRACULOUS CURES AT LOURDES

It was July 3, 1947 when Madame Rose Martin took three baths at the famous shrine in France. She weighed 70 pounds. In February of that year she had surgery for cancer of the uterus. Several operations followed that one, but the cancer continued to spread. Madame Rose was a terminal case.

When she returned to her hotel room after the baths, she discovered that the frightful pain she had endured for so long was gone. Her appetite suddenly was ravenous. Several other medical complications vanished. Months later the Lourdes medical bureau examined Rose Martin and declared the woman free of cancer. She had gained 34 pounds and had become healthy looking and full of vitality. The healing was confirmed by more than 20 doctors and surgeons.

On May 3, 1949 the Bishop of Nice acted at the request of the Lourdes Medical Commission and declared Rose Martin's healing to be a miraculous cure.

Simone Rams, 15, arrived at Lourdes on May 12, 1959. She was in excruciating pain. The girl from Belgium had been suffering with cancer of the thigh bone ever since 1951. An operation confirmed the diagnosis. Miss Rams' left thigh had been swollen now for nine years, and by the time she was taken to Lourdes she was considered by her doctors to be a completely hopeless case. In fact, they gave her only a few days to live.

Simone made the trip to Lourdes on a stretcher, with a doctor and nurse in attendance. On May 18,1959 her pain grew worse. She knew she had to get to the baths quickly. She had been lying in her hotel room for six days to gain strength, but now she had to get to the shrine.

When she entered the miraculous waters she knew her troubles were over. She felt health surging through her. The doctor in attendance was stunned by the fact that the huge swelling on her thigh had vanished! He asked her to take a few steps. She did so.

Simone had not walked in years! That afternoon and evening she consumed enormous amounts of food. Simone Rams had rarely eaten full meals before.

After two years of extensive tests on the girl, her cure was accepted as a miracle by the Lourdes Medical Board.

THE IRISH "LOURDES"

Just before the turn of the century the villagers of Knock in County Mayo, Ireland, were in the throes of a terrible famine. Many were so weak from hunger they could hardly walk. Nevertheless, 15 of the villagers made their to their Catholic church to pray for deliverance.

At one end of the small church a light began to form. The parishioners looked at it in amazement. When the light became brilliant they were able to distinguish the figures of the Virgin Mary, St. Joseph and St. John. The forms stood at the church's altar. They looked up at a lamb surrounded by golden stars.

The vision was reported immediately. Villagers with diseases came to church and claimed miraculous cures. Authorities from the Roman Catholic Church came to Knock to investigate the claims. Villagers were interrogated for several days. The authorities were not convinced about the cures, but they did feel that the 15 villagers had seen a vision.

Since that time the Church may have changed its mind. Today, Knock is known as the "Irish Lourdes" because so many cures have taken place there.

For example, Nicholas Doyle of Bray County was 10 years old when he went to the shrine. He was stricken with rheumatic fever. Doctors told him that his heart was so weak from the disease that he should stay confined to his bed most of the time. A few days after he was blessed in the small church he was seen riding his bicycle. His family doctor was unable to explain what had caused the rheumatic fever to disappear.

Bridie Hopkins is another example. This Leeds teenager was taken to Knock with a diseased leg bone. Her entire leg was numb. After she received a blessing at the shrine, the numbness was gone. A week later, doctors who had discovered the leg bone disease declared that she was completely healed.

ITALY'S "LOURDES"

The Madonna statue was a foot high and exactly like thousands of other such statues that are cheaply made in a plant in Sicily. It was made of plaster and was hollow. It sold for three dollars.

This particular Madonna was given to Antionetta and Angelo Iannuso of Syracuse, Sicily, as a wedding present. It was spring, 1953. Antionetta was a devoutly religious girl. Angelo was a communist sympathizer.

A few months later, Antionetta became pregnant and had an especially hard time of it. Pain wracked her body. She could hardly see. The 20-year-old girl prayed to the Madonna for release from the pain and torment. During the morning of August 29, 1953 the pain was especially excruciating. She turned to the Madonna for help and saw that the statue was weeping!

The girl thought she had lost her mind. When she explained what she saw later, no one believed her; not even her husband, mother and sister-in-law. Angelo removed the Madonna and unscrewed the base to show his wife that there was nothing inside. The wall behind the statue was perfectly dry. But when the Madonna was placed in her wall niche everyone saw two small tears form in its eyes.

Within a few short days everyone in Italy had heard about the weeping Madonna. Syracuse, an Ionian seaport city of some 60,000, was suddenly inundated with visitors to see the miracle.

The police department tried to hold back the crowds, then decided to move the statue to their headquarters for safety. A policeman carried the Madonna to a squad car and held it in his lap. When he arrived at headquarters his uniform was drenched with the

Madonna's tears. One detective caught several of the tears in a vial and brought them to the crime laboratory for analysis. The result: They were human tears!

Soon after Antionetta saw the tears for the first time, her agonizing pains disappeared. Others were cured, as well. The ritual was to brush the victim with cloth wetted by the Madonna's tears. A three-year-old girl with polio was taken to the Madonna. After a brushing she was able to move her arm for the first time since her illness.

A girl struck dumb eleven years earlier was brought to the Madonna and had her mouth brushed with the tear-stained cloth. The girl immediately began to talk.

All of the initial cures occurred during a four-day period. On the fourth day the tears stopped. The statue was then carried through the streets of Syracuse in front of a procession of 30,000 persons. The Madonna was placed in a glass-walled case.

Today, the shrine is located on a 12-acre site. There is room enough for 20,000 pilgrims. The Madonna no longer cries, but there is plenty of evidence that she still works her healing miracles. Crutches, canes and braces can be seen near the little statue.

MIRACLE HEALING: HOW IS IT PROVED?

The best way to answer that question is to study the healing Grotto of Bernadette at Lourdes, France. The shrine here was constructed on the spot where Bernadette Soubirous talked with the Virgin Mary in 1858. Since that miracle, pilgrims have journeyed to Lourdes to seek salvation and healing from the natural spring in the hillside.

Each year some 200,000 persons visit the shrine. In 1958, when Lourdes celebrated its 100th anniversary, more than two million pilgrims arrived. It is a small community and it was hard-pressed to accommodate everyone.

The miracles that have occurred at the Grotto are well-documented. They have been declared as paranormal cures. Of course,

thousands who have immersed themselves in the spring water claim they have been cured, but the Lourdes Medical Bureau has been able to certify only 54 miraculous cures since 1858. The Bureau has set up a criteria, which is followed assiduously.

1. The affliction must be a serious disease. If it is not curable, it must be very difficult to cure.

2. There must be no improvement in the patient's condition prior to the visit to the Lourdes shrine.

3. Medication that may have been used must have been ineffective.

4. The cure must be totally complete.

5. The cure must be unquestionably definitive and free of all doubt.

These rules are rigid, but they have to be. Certainly, thousands of people have left their canes and crutches at the shrine, but no cure is considered miraculous unless the church has seen to it that the patient has passed this strict test before being certified.

THE MIRACLES OF ORAL ROBERTS

The Pentacostal Holiness minister, Oral Roberts, has appeared regularly on hundreds of radio stations and television shows. He has launched worldwide crusades and has practiced the ancient art of "the laying on of hands" and prayer on thousands of sufferers. What is not generally known about Reverend Roberts is that he was the recipient of a miracle in his younger days.

Oral was a sickly child without the strength to pick cotton or help with the chores on his parents' farm in Pontotac County, Oklahoma. He also stuttered so horribly that he was ashamed to face visitors.

At the age of 16 he was playing basketball in Atoka, Oklahoma when he suddenly collapsed on the court. He lay writhing in pain. Blood spewed from his mouth. Rushed home to bed, he told

his father, who was a preacher as well as a farmer, "Papa, I've gone the last mile of the way... ."

During the next six months his weight dropped from 160 to 118 pounds. He could no longer use his legs. Then one night "The Lindsay Saints," a touring group of Evangelists from Lindsay, Oklahoma, stayed with Oral all night, praying for him. In the morning, Oral was able to walk.

A short time later, doctors told the boy's family that Oral had tuberculosis. He was at a gospel tent meeting one night, sitting on a padded chair, when the healing part of the ceremony began.

Brother George Moncey placed his hands on Oral's shoulders and ordered the sickness to leave the boy's lungs. Oral leaped from the chair crying that he was healed. To prove it, he ran around the seats without losing his breath. He also had a bonus in that his stuttering defect was cured as well.

Reverend Roberts has performed an untold number of miraculous healings, but one of the most dramatic occurred when he had been preaching for about 10 years. The deacon of the Toccoa church dropped an automobile motor on his foot. The man's name was Clyde Lawson and he was screaming in pain when Oral Roberts approached. The foot, apparently, was mutilated. Blood gushed through the man's shoe. Reverend Roberts knelt beside the man and prayed. Suddenly, the pain stopped. Lawson took off his shoe and saw that his foot was perfectly normal.

According to Reverend Roberts, he received a call from God shortly after the incident. He said he was lying on the floor when he heard the command: "Get on your feet! Drive your car one block and turn right."

Reverend Roberts felt that the voice was God's. He obeyed the order and found a downtown auditorium that was not being used. The city was Enid, Oklahoma. He rented it for healing services.

The voice again commanded him: "You will heal the sick from this moment on and cast out devils by my powers."

That was the beginning of Roberts' great work as a healer. He insists again and again, at every service, "Only God can heal."

THE HAND OF GOD IS CAPABLE OF REACHING DOWN AND TOUCHING ALL OF US.

Notice the phrase "is capable" in the title. Why didn't we simply say, "The Hand of God Reaches Down and Touches All of Us?" The answer is not at all profound. What makes Him capable of touching all of us is prayer. Nothing more, nothing less.

How can God know that we need Him unless we pray? If He doesn't hear from us then He must assume that we are all right, that we are not in trouble, that we don't ail physically or mentally.

And we don't have to go into lengthy explanations to define prayer. It is nothing more than our way of communicating with God. It is a medium, just as newspapers, radio and television are mediums. Those outlets communicate with us. We are receptive when we buy a newspaper or turn on our radio or TV.

God is receptive when we open our hearts to Him in prayer.

CALL TO PRAYER

We've heard all sorts of phrases about prayer. "The family that prays together stays together." "Prayer changes things." "Pray about it." Those phrases are fine, but they really don't mean anything in today's world. The unfortunate thing is that we have forgotten how to pray—if we ever knew how to in the first place.

You have seen examples of the lost art of prayer time again. The little child who kneels beside her bed and recites, "Now I lay me down to sleep." And how about the devout churchgoers who kneel in a pew and recite the Lord's Prayer over and over again in a never-ending monotonous drone?

For examples of true heartfelt prayer, listen closely to your

priest or minister the next time you are in church. He does not mouth meaningless words, but speaks eloquently to God with deep feelings, and certainly touches every area of human need. You can see other examples in those who sit quietly by the seashore, or under a tree, and do nothing more than admire life and nature. They are praying, too, although they may not be aware of it because they are not asking God for anything. They are merely appreciating what He has given them.

THE PURPOSE OF PRAYER

You may hear someone say, "I don't pray much anymore because I don't have any serious problems." That statement is a good example of how far we've strayed from the art of prayer. The person is saying, "I don't need a miracle, so why should I bother God for one? I'm doing all right. I'm healthy. I've got enough money. My future looks bright."

Certainly, problems may be solved through prayers, but that is not the primary purpose of communing with God. The real purpose of prayer is to lift yourself to a high level of consciousness. At a high level you can be conditioned in mind and body so that the hand of God can reach down to touch you. At a high level of consciousness you will find yourself closer to the real substance and intelligence of God.

Jesus said, "Ye seek me, not because ye saw the miracles, but because ye did eat of the loaves, and were filled. Labor not for the meat which perisheth, but for the meat which endureth unto everlasting life. God is Spirit and they that worship must worship in Spirit and in Truth." (John 6:26, 27). What He is telling us is that we must work to change the image of Jesus as a miracle worker and an entity who has all of the answers for us.

He asks us not to pray because we know we will be seen praying. He asks us not to pray because we think we should be praying. He doesn't want you to pray so that your lumbago will be healed, or so that you may get a better job. What He wants you to do is to pray for that higher level of consciousness, pray "and all things shall be added unto you."

A MIRACLE A MINUTE
With Candle Burning Prayers For A Good And Prosperous Life

What that last phrase means is that you don't have to spell out your problems to Him. Once you have established a true communication with Him, He will understand your earthly agonies and alleviate them.

PRAYER IS NOT A BUSINESS DEAL

You don't say, "God, get me out this mess and I promise I'll become a member of the clergy, or I'll donate a lot of money to charity."

You can't strike bargains with God. That's not the way to do it. Nor is it reasonable to be put off because God does not answer your prayers. Some of us whine by saying, "I go to church every Sunday. I give to the poor. I pray twice a day and I don't do anything bad. So why doesn't God answer my prayers? Why doesn't He give me what I ask for?"

The answer is simple. The whiner did not do all of those good things because he was really looking for the inner communion with God, but because he felt them a sense of duty.

And how many times have you been pressured by a salesman who flatters you because he wants your business? If you think that will work with God, you' are wrong. With God, flattery will get you nowhere. You can't expect the Lord to be moved by praise. You can't expect Him to listen to coaxing and pleading. You can't shout at Him, or indulge in vain repetition. Nor can you pray seemingly forever and expect results. God is not capricious. He is not reluctant. If you expect Him to touch you, you must learn the technique of prayer.

THE KEY TO UNDERSTANDING

Eric Butterworth wrote in his definitive book, "***Discover the Power Within You,***" an easy technique for achieving that elusive oneness with God. It's worth studying. "Prayer is not something we do to God but to ourselves. It is not a position but a disposition. It is not flattery but a sense of oneness. It is not asking but knowing. It is not words but feeling. It is not will but willingness."

There is nothing mysterious about those words. Many people who have mastered the art of prayer would agree with them even though they have never put their own similar thoughts into words. We know, for instance, that George Washington achieved a oneness with God when he prayed for his men at Valley Forge. Abraham Lincoln prayed often, but never for himself. Albert Einstein, perhaps the greatest mind the world ever produced, was an ardent believer in prayer. He was convinced that the law of the universe is a force for good, and that we can achieve a oneness with it by thought and prayer.

DON'T BLAME YOURSELF
FOR NOT KNOWING HOW TO PRAY

Most of us have grown up with two strikes against us. When we were young we were told to study, but no one ever told us how to study. It's the same with prayer. We were told to pray, but not told how to pray. So we did what everyone else did (which was wrong), and read prayers from books, or followed a priest's or minister's words from an altar, or we memorized standard prayers not really knowing what the meaning of those prayers was.

If you felt frustrated, you can take some consolation in the fact that you were not alone. At times, even clergymen felt that way. In fact, famed Bishop John Robinson had a sense of frustration along these lines, and even a sense of guilt.

He wrote: "I believe the experts have induced in us a deep inferiority complex. They tell us that this is the way we ought to pray, and yet we find that we cannot maintain ourselves for any length of time even on the lowest rung of the ladder, let alone climb it. We are evidently not 'the praying type.' And so we carry on with an unacknowledged sense of failure and guilt. I can testify to this most strongly from the time I spent in a theological college, both as a student and as a teacher. Here was a laboratory for prayer. Here one ought to be able to pray, if ever one could. If one failed in these circumstances, what hope was there later on when one was surrounded and sucked down by 'the world'? And, yet, I believe I am not alone

in finding a theological college the most difficult rather than the easiest place in which to pray. In fact, I know I am not. For I discovered there what I can only describe as a freemasonry of silent, profoundly discouraged, underground opposition, which felt that all that was said and written about prayer was doubtless unexceptional but simply did not speak to 'our' condition. But nothing else' was offered in its place, and to this day, we have an inferiority complex. We dare not admit to others or to ourselves what non-starters we are."

DON'T BE A NON-STARTER

Bishop Robinson, admitted a failing most of us have. We want to pray, but we find that other things intrude, or we don't have time for it. Of course, that's nonsense. We do have time to do the things that come easy for us, like watching television, or going to a movie. We have time to chat with our friends and neighbors. We have time to listen to music, or go to dances. But we don't have time to pray.

The really devout don't have this problem. They set aside a few minutes in each day for prayer. It might be early in the morning when the house is quiet. It might be in bed at night, just before sleep comes. It might even be during a quiet period at their jobs.

The important point is that they do make the time for prayer, even snatching a few moments from an incredibly busy schedule. Prayer has become so much a part of their lives that it is as important to them as eating and sleeping, and yet they do it totally without ostentation. You may have a friend or two, or maybe more, who pray often, but in secret. They have no desire to brag about it, or to let you find them at it.

Jesus said it all in His "Sermon on the Mount." "Take heed that ye do not your righteousness before men, to be seen of them: else ye have no reward with your Father who is in Heaven. When therefore thou doest alms, sound not a trumpet before thee, as the hypocrites do in the synagogues and in the streets, that they may have glory of men. Verily I say unto you, They have received their reward. But when thou doest alms, let not thy left hand know what thy right hand doeth; that thine alms may be in secret: and thy Fa-

ther who seeth in secret shall recompense thee. And when ye pray, ye shall not be as the hypocrites: for they love to stand and pray in the synagogues and in the corners of the streets, that they may be seen of men. Verily I say unto you, they have received their reward. But thou, when thou prayest, enter into thine inner chamber, and having shut thy door, pray to thy Father who is in secret, and thy Father who seeth in secret shall recompense thee (Matt. 6: 1-6)

JESUS' WORDS

Jesus says it very clearly in the "Sermon on the Mount." If you pray to be seen praying by others, you will receive your reward, which is, quite simply, notice from others. If you pray in secret, your Father will recompense you, and that, too, is clear. You will truly receive what you are praying for.

Jesus also says that we are thinking beings. The only connection between us and God is our minds. We can reach Him only through our consciousness. Our thoughts, not words, in His direction must be spiritually oriented. We must think positively. We must concentrate.

DIVINE LAW

What is divine law? Can we see it, feel it, hear it? The answer is no. Divine law is a nonmaterial force. It cannot be seen, felt, heard. But you may well ask: How can I be sure it exists? The answer to that is in the form of other questions: Can you see the wind? Can you see electricity? There are a lot of things we can't see, but we know they exist. The same can be said of divine law. We can't see God, but we know He exists in everything; that is alive. We know the love of God because we can see love in ourselves. We see God's wisdom in the intelligence of man. So when Jesus says "The Father who is in secret," He means that we must pray to Him even though we can't see Him.

Nor should His secrecy surprise us. We are surrounded by secrets. The acorn in the ground does its work of growing into an

oak tree without the prying eyes of man. We push a light switch and a room is illuminated. Secret? To many of us it is. The same can be said of a picture that appears on a television screen, or the voice we hear on the telephone.

They are all secrets to many of us only because we never bothered to find out why they happen. And it is the same with those who pray to God. They have unlocked the secret of communication with God. They have reached a higher consciousness because they have tried again and again until they succeeded.

And it must be pointed out that these people are no smarter than we are. They are not "gifted." Their only distinction is that they have taken the trouble to find out what prayer is all about, and how they can receive the "recompense" that Jesus talks about in His "Sermon on the Mount."

SHOULD WE PRAY FOR MIRACLES?

How often have you heard someone say, "I'm praying for a miracle to happen?" Actually, trying to make miracles happen is not the purpose of prayer. The hand of God will touch us if we learn how to pray, and some astounding things may occur, but they will only be the manifestations of the unity between God and us. This is called the divine law of fulfillment.

In actuality, when we ask for a miracle in prayer, we are really limiting the power of prayer. There is no need for a miracle. We may ask for good health, prosperity or guidance. All right, if we get them after prayer it merely means that God is fulfilling His designs for us in the first place. Health, prosperity and guidance comprise the nature of God. Those are the things He wants for His ideal creation, which is man.

"MAKE NO PARADE OF YOUR RELIGION"

Jesus spoke those words and referred to the "hypocrites" who prayed in synagogues and on street corners. By "hypocrite" He was talking about the religious zealot who makes a splashy show of his devoutness and his prayer. Jesus, however, did not condemn the

individual, only the practice.

What Jesus could not have known at the time was that too many of us would be handed our religion as a custom-made entity. We were to wear certain garments. There, would be certain prayers to learn by rote, certain devotions to attend to, religious ceremonies. That's all well and good, but if these rites don't open our hearts to God, if we don't find that oneness with the Almighty, then obviously the sacred ceremonies are reduced to nothing more than social functions.

We do need our houses of worship. They are the places at which we can gather to find peace; quiet places in which to sincerely pray, and the suggestion here is to go to them as often as you can; not only when services are being held, but when the churches are empty, and when you can sit down alone and bow your head in prayer.

Unfortunately, not all of us can do that. For some mysterious reason we need the parades and pageantry. But that was not the way Jesus thought of religion. He didn't see it as a congregation of people praying together; He saw it as one individual, alone, reaching out with his heart and his thoughts, raising his level of consciousness with no one looking at him. Jesus saw it as a one-on-one relationship. If you are a devout churchgoer, which you should be, think of yourself as being alone in the church next time. Just God and you. Blot out those around you. If you have trouble doing that, remain in church for a few minutes after everyone else is gone. Relax. Lift your thoughts. Who knows, you may then learn what the power of prayer is all about.

"SELF-RELIANCE"

Ralph Waldo Emerson wrote a classic essay about prayer, titled Reliance." It is only one paragraph, but worth repeating here:

"Prayer looks abroad and asks for some foreign addition to come through some foreign virtue, and loses itself in endless mazes of natural and supernatural, and mediatorial and miraculous. Prayer that craves a particular commodity, anything less than all good, is vicious. Prayer is the contemplation of the facts of life from the highest point of view. It is the soliloquy of a beholding and jubilant soul. It is the spirit of God pronouncing His works good. But prayer as a means to effect a private end is meanness and theft. It supposes dualism and not unity in nature and consciousness. As soon as the man is at one with God, he will not beg. He will then see prayer in all action."

"AND IN PRAYING USE NOT VAIN REPETITIONS"

Those are Jesus' words and the word "vain" is quite important here and Jesus used it because He had no intention of condemning ordinary repetition, only vain repetition. You must remember that on one occasion Jesus Himself said one prayer three times.

What is the difference between repetition and vain repetition? The answer lies in intent. If you repeat a prayer over and over

again in an effort to strengthen your mind with thoughts of God, then there is no quarrel at all with repetition. If, however, you repeat prayers with the idea that you are conditioning God to your needs, then you are being vain. You have to remember in your prayers that you are trying to lift your consciousness, not God's.

A PUZZLING QUESTION

Matthew made the statement in 6:8, and it has puzzled Christians for eons. He said: "Your Father knoweth what things ye have need of, before ye ask Him." On the surface, it doesn't make sense to pray for anything if God already knows what your problems are. Why ask?

The tragedy is that we have forgotten that important statement by Matthew. If we had it tacked up on a wall near the spot in which we pray, it would alter our thoughts on the subject.

And with the statement on the wall, you could add the phrase, "God is spirit," and that would answer that age-old question for you.

God is spirit. He is the Supreme Being. We can't give Him human qualities when we pray to Him. When you do that you are already thinking negatively. You don't have to ask for things when you have raised up your thoughts in an effort at unity with God. Remember:

God is life. Why ask God for life? You are the projection of that life, except that you are visible. God is wisdom. Why ask God for wisdom? Your mind is an extension of the infinite mind of God. God inspires. You receive that inspiration. If it stops, don't blame God; blame yourself. What must be done then is to reestablish yourself with God. The Mind of God is in you. You can be at one with it by conscious effort.

The same can be said of healing. We pray fervently to be healed. But do we lift up our thoughts? Do we become aware of the wholeness of life? We ask to be healed without really accepting the fact that God is the wholeness of life. How can we ask God to accept begging when the individual doing the begging has no thought of

trying to lift himself up spiritually?

Now when we read Matthew's statement we see it in a different light. We are a little closer to the real meaning of prayer. But we still have a way to go.

THE WORDS OF LUKE (12:32)

"It is the Father's good pleasure to give you the kingdom."

The Almighty wants nothing more than to give you what you pray for. But to get it you have to do something for yourself. It is something that God won't do for you and it is the act of getting into the Spirit. Elevate your thoughts to God. Believe in Him. Jesus said: "All things whatsoever ye pray and ask for, believe that ye receive them, and ye shall have them."

The key phrase in Jesus' sentence above is "believe that ye receive them." That appears to be a contradiction in terms. If you already believe that you have what you are asking for, then why ask?

But think about what Jesus said for a moment. Think about God's plan for us. As a spiritual being, He has already given us the Kingdom, and it resides within us. He has seen to it that we are self-sufficient, that we have all of the built-in capacities to reach the goal of being a total person. You already have all of the resources you need at your command. All you need do is to pray for a release of your spiritual reserves. Draw upon these reserves by uniting yourself with God.

"BE STILL AND KNOW THAT I AM GOD."

These words can be found in Psalms 46:10 and they tell us much about how to pray. "Be still" simply means to shut yourself up alone, shut out the world's concerns, shut out all petty annoyances. "And know that I am God" means to reaffirm your beliefs in the Almighty. When you pray to Him you know you must reach down into the depths of your being so that you can understand better the truth of your relationship with God. Be still, be quiet, be calm. This is a truly silent period for you.

There is no need for entreaty or supplication. Those things

should be behind you. And, yes, even adoration. God knows you adore Him; you don't have to keep reminding Him of that fact. What He would rather see you do during your quiet period is to let your heart speak the language of your soul.

When you express your gratitude for what you have, that's all the praise God wants. When you reach out for the spirit of reverence, God knows you adore Him.

PRAYING IS NO EASY JOB

When you begin your new program of daily prayers you are likely to find that concentration can be difficult. Other thoughts will intrude. You will have to keep returning to your mission. But don't be concerned about it. Meditation in the beginning can be extremely difficult for anyone. The only important thing is that you remember to return your thoughts to God.

VISUALIZATION HELPS

While praying, try to visualize that you already have what you are asking for. This is especially helpful if you are praying for good health, or are praying to maintain the good health you already have.

Visualization is nothing more than picturing your own body in perfect health. First you study the physical and medical aspects of the problem, then picture yourself totally free from the consequences of the problem.

God is the personification of positive thinking. In prayer, no matter what your reason for praying, you are engaged in positive thinking. Visualizing yourself with your wish granted, you are eliminating negative thinking completely.

MAKE PRAYER A HABIT

Before you go to work in the morning, take a moment or two to get your thoughts in tune to the Infinite Mind. Remind yourself that you are a spiritual being and that the Kingdom of God is within you. If you can't find time during the day to pray, then use a small part of your evening to it, or at bedtime. The ideal is to spend about 15 minutes in prayer, three times a day. Once the habit is established firmly in your routine, you will go to your inner chamber almost automatically. And every time you go there the concentration, the meditation process, will be that much easier to accomplish.

MIRACLES ARE ACCOMPLISHABLE
– ESPECIALLY WHEN YOU ADD A PRAYER
AND A CANDLE

By Maria D' Andrea

I am sure we have all gone through periods of loneliness and grief, perhaps caused by a crisis, an illness or even death. Out of despair we may have gotten down on our knees and prayed to God for guidance and a miracle to happen in our lives.

Many of us may feel disappointed that our prayers to God have gone mostly unanswered.

Is it possible that we are not following the necessary "procedures" which will enable God to hear our call? Is there more to harvesting a miracle than just getting down on our knees and stretching out our hands in praise to the Lord, thereby having our demands met?

I believe that the power of prayer is the strongest defense we have against individual hardships in our lives. Look back at your life as a child and you will notice that what you asked for – prayed for – often manifested itself, maybe not as fast as you would have liked . . . but a response did come forth. So what are you doing wrong now?

I like to tell people that visualization will ramp up the reaction you are likely to get from the cosmos. And, in order to intensify the visualization process, I have come to understand that several things are of tremendous help in projecting your prayers with super speed

into the higher realms:

1. Choosing the proper prayer – one that is quite specific to your petition to the Almighty.

2. The time (day) you select to send forth your prayer for help creates the necessary vibrations to get a positive answer.

3. Candles are important in any spiritual ritual. Burning a specific colored candle alongside you when you pray will light the way to a positive conclusion to your prayers.

4. And burning incense will send your message directly to Heaven. There are specific incenses that will aid in obtaining the desired results, depending on the prayers you wish to have recognized.

As you begin to pray, concentrate on sending your message out into the universe.

Think of God as a magnificent ball of White Light. Next, think of numerous beams of White Light – such as laser beams – coming from this ball. At the end of each beam, visualize a smaller ball or spark of White Light. Each spark of Light is a person, a soul. We are all directly connected to the Godhead. We are all part of Him. We are co-creators of our world, our reality.

Though we may be limited in our lives, God isn't limited at all!

Whatever thought we put our mind to we will make manifest. On a security level, this is the strongest force known. Even if you do not know any form of psychical protection, prayer alone will protect you. You can use a prayer you already know or make one up yourself. Prayers are very effective as long as you mean what you are saying or thinking from the heart and have faith in the Lord. If you ask to be protected, He will do so. You will be 100 percent taken care of. God

does not make mistakes. Many cultures are aware of this and put this knowledge to practical use.

It does not matter if you call Him God, Buddha, Father Sky or whatever Supreme Being you place your faith in. Whatever name you use, it stands for the One Source we can all put our faith into.

Prayers come in various forms. Poetry is well known, verse, reading a particular Psalm, talking to God. Any form of communication you feel comfortable with will activate the spark that unites us to Him.

Saying the words mentally does work. However, speaking the words out loud gives them more power. Even if you whisper, the sound goes out. There is a force behind the vibration of your voice that resonates with the Divine.

What I have done to magnify and enhance the outcome of your prayers is to add candles, incense and the best times to work with these principialities to magnify and deepen the outcome being focused on. Individual prayers all work with their own vibrations, and all energy is united/connected to increasing the power of our prayers and repelling all negativity in our lives.

The more we add a positive energy to our request the better. Think of prayers in terms of a battery charger for a car. The car is running slowly but still works to get you to your destination. But when you charge the battery, it speeds up and gets you there even faster.

In this respect, each candle color has its own purpose and vibration, just as each incense type manifests itself in a unique spiritual quality. Furthermore, the best day to start working on your intent comes from a combination of factors, such as the effects of the sun, moon, planets and the spirits at our disposal in your life.

There are numerous cultural approaches to praying. Native Americans view Him as the Great Spirit or Father Sky. We must know

that we are all connected. There is a saying, "May God Be With You," which correlates to **_Legyen Veled Az Isten_** in Hungarian, which is my native language. In Hungary they believe in "Isten," which is the Hungarian word for God.

So focus specifically on your intentions. Speak with determination. And, above all else, use the spiritual tools given here to improve your life . . . and a Miracle A Minute may soon be yours!

BONUS CANDLE BURNING PRAYERS FOR A GOOD AND PROSPEROUS LIFE

by Maria D'Andrea

PRAYER FOR PROTECTION
Children especially

This is an ancient prayer used by adepts and passed down through generations. This one is especially good for children to say as a night time prayer:

There are four corners on my bed,

There are four angels at the head,

Matthew, Mark, Luke and John,

Please Bless this bed that I lay on.

Amen

Proper Candle: Light a White candle, any size and let it burn completely out.

Proper Incense: Light Tobacco or Frankincense and let it burn out.

Proper Day: Start on a Sunday night. Every night is great to start.

* * * * *

PRAYER FOR PROTECTION FROM EVIL AT NIGHT

Say this prayer as you light the candle and incense on the correct day to magnify the power:

God protect me through the night,

Through the negative energies that try to bind,

In the name of the Father, the Son and the Holy Spirit,

Let the White Light of God enfold me within it.

Amen

Proper Candle: White or gold. Utilize one or both.

Proper Incense: Bayberry or Frankincense with Myrrh (Myrrh should never be used by itself)

Proper Day: Sunday or Friday

* * * * *

PRAYER FOR WISHES FULFILLED

Write a letter to God as a prayer. Make it in a letter form as follows:

Dear God,

Please hear my prayer. I wish to manifest (fill in whatever your desires are). I manifest this now through your help.

In a positive way, to harm none.

I trust in you and know that as I ask, it is already set in motion and my prayer is answered.

Thank you Father.

Love,

(Sign your name)

Put the letter in your Bible or on your bed, between your mattress and box spring. Leave it there until your wish manifests, then burn the letter and throw the ashes outside, back to the wind.

Proper Candle: Orange or white. You can use both at the same time.

Proper Incense: Sandalwood or violet

Proper Day: Friday

* * * * *

PRAYER FOR HELP

1-   You can pray Psalm # 86 and concentrate on the area in which you need the help. Know that help is coming.

1-   Speak this prayer with focus and sincerity:

Lord, my God I seek thy power,

Help me in this time of trouble,

Show me the Light that shines this hour,

To cancel blocks that overpower.

I am standing on the promises,

As God has given,

To hear my heart,

He now comes to deliver.

AMEN

Proper Candle: Blue

Proper Incense: Rose

Proper Day: Sunday

* * * * *

PRAYER FOR NEW LOVE

Love comes in many forms. There is romantic love, family love, friendship love, love of a pet, love of a location where you like to live, love of a type of environment (lakes, forests and so on), and other situations where love comes in to play.

This prayer is for romantic love:

I pray for love to come to me,

For both of us most speedily.

Our hearts prepared; the time is right

Guide love to me with grace and Light.

Amen

Proper Candle: Pink or red

Proper Incense: Iris or rose or patchouli

Proper Day: Friday or Sunday

* * * * *

PRAYER FOR HEALING

This prayer speeds up your natural healing process. Remember God has unlimited power. Picture yourself in perfect health and pray the following with trust:

Candle green I now declare,

Gods color I now manifest,

To send me healing I now intend,

Through His power I now manifest.

Through earth and fire,

Through water and air,

Come to me healing,

I so demand.

Thank you Father.

Proper Candle: Green

Proper Incense: Sandalwood

Proper Day: Monday

* * * * *

PRAYER FOR BUSINESS TO GROW

As you focus your intent on your business growing, picture / visualize your business as a small ball of green light. Take a few deep breaths and with each breath, see this ball (of your business) getting bigger with each breath. After a few breaths, when you feel comfortable, light the candle and incense and say the prayer sincerely.

As above, so below,

My business now begins to grow.

From east to west,

From north to south,

My business explodes all around.

Today brings in abundant joy,

I see prosperity now grows and grows.

My heart can see what others need,

And so I sow some brand new seeds.

And so it is, Amen

When you put back to others-it can be giving someone a ride to work, helping lift a heavy package for them or simply giving advice to help (it isn't always money)- it comes back stronger to you. What you put out, good, bad or indifferent, comes back-it is a universal spiritual Law. It works as long as you do it from the heart.

Proper Candle: Red or orange

Proper Incense: Success or Blessings or sage

Proper Day: Tuesday

* * * * *

PRAYER TO RELEASE ANGER

At times, we have valid reasons or imagined ones for holding onto our anger. However, that is not healthy for us. Why should we let others or situations get the best of us? We can rise above it and be healthy, happy, peaceful and victorious.

It is time to reclaim your power and release the anger. Say the following prayer:

Through the Power of the Divine, I now release all blocks to my peaceful life.

I call the angels to banish stress, anger, regrets and any obstacles from my Divine Right to be happy, joyous and victorious.

In the battle to gain my victory, I now release all negative, vengeful thoughts and feelings and replace them with the Power of Light.

With God at my side, no obstacle is too big.

So be it.

Proper Candle: White

Proper Incense: Tobacco or jasmine or honeysuckle

Proper Day: Sunday

* * * * *

PRAYER FOR LUCK

The vibration of attracting luck into your life increases when you do the following prayers:

1- Pray Psalm # 65 once a week. You also need to work on an ethical level and be open to opportunities. Burn a purple candle with Frankincense.

2- Say:

Magnetic powers come to me,

Through earth and air,

Through fire and sea.

My life becomes a magnet now,

My heart a fountain of flowing love.

My mind creates all that I need,

Attracting abundance at maximum speed.

Like the rain sustains the tree,

Lucky life now comes to me.

Proper Candle: Orange or blue or green

Proper Incenses: Lucky Lady or Fast Luck or Magnet

Proper Day: Thursday

* * * * *

PRAYER FOR MEETING NEW PEOPLE

Sometimes, we just simply need new people in our lives.

Pray this prayer:

Archangel Michael up above send good people into my life, so that my life will be Blessed. I now start living the qualities I look for in others. I am loving, spiritual, ethical, trustworthy, (fill in qualities you are looking for) and positive. So I now attract people who are the same.

As the ancient Laws of attraction say- "Like attracts like". I now put forth my plea, help to bring happiness unto me.

Thank you. So be it.

Proper Candle: Yellow or gold

Proper Incense: High John or rose

Proper Day: Sunday

* * * * *

SPIRITUAL PURSUITS

There are so many forms of spiritual pursuits. Meditation, heightening or developing your awareness or abilities, finding out what your abilities are, looking into psychic / intuitive insights, religion, history, metaphysics, and so much more.

Invoke the Archangel with this prayer:

Archangel Arcan blessings on thee,

Come to my aid and elevate me,

Entry to Higher Realms I seek,

To grow in spirit as meant to be.

As my helper on this plane,

Guide me to the Eternal Flame,

Let me not wrong turns to make,

Spiritual life now awaits.

So be it.

Proper Candle: White or purple or silver

Proper Incense: High John The Conqueror or Frankincense with Myrrh (never use Myrrh without Frankincense)

Proper Day: Monday

* * * * *

PRAYER TO HEIGHTEN CREATIVITY

Creativity comes in many forms. Outward abilities can be a painter, musician, architect, writer, poet and inwardly it can be an inventor (after all, somebody invented the light bulb), a concept person, a creative mind, among other creative pursuits.

This prayer is meant to help in elevating those creative abilities already within you. It is as though you are watering a seed within yourself to grow.

Say the following prayer:

Angels, angels come to me,

Circle round me lovingly,

Through inspiration, dreams and such,

Heighten creativity from above.

As a child of God,

I am inspired,

Bring forth my spark,

Send me my desire.

Thank you Creativity Angels.

Proper Candle: Light blue or orange

Proper Incense: Magnet or orange

Proper Day: Wednesday

* * * * *

PRAYER FOR LEGAL ISSUES

Legal situations can be very difficult, including on emotional levels. This prayer will increase them to be more in your favor. Remember, God is always at your side.

Say this prayer:

I now invoke the Guardians of Justice.

Help set things right and in my favor. I claim my right to cosmic justice, peace from this situation and joy at the results.

I know that as I ask God and my Guardians, it is already being worked on. God and the Guardians know what is in my heart and that truth and justice are on my side.

I now claim my Right and it is now so.

Thank you God and thank you my Guardians.

Now, after saying this prayer, know in your heart that it is set into motion and do not worry about the outcome or stress. When you do so, it slows the process down.

It is as though you asked a friend to go to the store for you and then you constantly called to see where he / she is. It slowed down your friend every time the phone had to be answered.

Relax and trust in the outcome.

Proper Candle: Brown or gold

Proper Incense: Tobacco or High John or Success

Proper Day: Saturday

* * * * *

PRAYER FOR PROTECTION POWER

In the Bible, in Job 11:18, it said, "God will protect you and give you rest".

Spiritual protection comes in all cultures. It is a powerful weapon.

Pray the following:

As above, so below. I acknowledge Divine Power is my Source.

I am NOW protected from all negativity through the Power of God. Nothing can harm me on any level. Through Divine Power, nothing can hurt my mind, body or soul. As I think this, I know it. So be it.

Thank you God.

Proper Candle: White or purple

Proper Incense: Blessings or mint or sage

Proper Day: Sunday

* * * * *

PRAYER FOR WHEN YOU ARE DEPRESSED

Depression can be very harmful emotionally and draining physically. We are meant to be happy and joyous. Realistically, we go through difficult situations and sometimes we need help to come out of that dark spot.

These prayers help to uplift you and help you get back on track quicker.

1-   Pray Psalm # 86 from your heart.

2-   Pray:

God of my ancestors, hear my words. I come to you in my time of need. I pray that this dark cloud is lifted from me Now. I know and trust that You are the Source of everything, so I know this is easy for you to change so I can regain my true spiritual self.

Who I really am is the spirit within me. I am spirit and want to be balanced and whole once again. Lift off this cloud, replace it with Divine energy so that I may honor you, help others and gain happiness in my life.

  I know that as I ask, it is done.

Thank you Lord. Amen.

Proper Candle: Red or white

Proper Incense: High John the Conqueror or any form of mint

Proper Day: Tuesday

* * * * *

PRAYER FOR LOVED ONES WHO PASSED

Pray this prayer with love in your heart:

Lord, giver of Light and Life, help my loved one have safe passage through the veil. Help to have (say the name of the person who passed) go through an easy transition and to have (name of loved one) go to his / her Happy Place.

Let (name of person) go Home to be with you, to a brighter, happier place. Let all grief, sorrow and pain be forgotten and joy and bliss replace it.

Even though he /she is truly missed, I know You hold him / her in Your hand. (Name of loved one) will always be in my heart and thoughts. May my sorrow at my loss not affect his / her journey into peace, love and Light.

Thank you Lord. Amen.

Proper Candle: White

Proper Incense: Lily or violet

Proper Day: Sunday

* * * * *

PRAYER FOR DECISIONS AND MENTAL INCREASE

Sometimes we need to heighten our mental senses. Such as at a time when you need to take a test or at a job interview. Pray this prayer:

Angels of Higher Intellect, come to my aid now .Help me to see the things I need. Help my decisions to come easily and readily. Make my mind aware and sharp, my concentration strong and my thoughts on the positive side.

My mind overflows with love and fairness. Help me to see all details, written or not. To see what I need to see to improve and better my life.

Thank you. So be it. Amen.

Proper Candle: Brown

Proper Incense: Musk or vanilla or mint

Proper Day: Wednesday

* * * * *

PRAYER FOR ABUNDANCE

Pray this prayer for all forms of abundance:

Abundance is my right from birth,

My Father ordained it to all concerned.

As I seek, so shall I find,

Untold treasured yet to come.

Unlimited, as grains of sand,

My storehouse to the rafters stand.

As I expect, so shall it be,

From sands of time to eternity.

This I decree. Thank you Lord. Amen

Proper Candle: Gold or purple or dark blue

Proper Incense: Seven Power or cinnamon or lavender

Proper Day: Sunday

* * * * *

PRAYER FOR ACHIEVING GOALS

Focus on your goal first in as much detail as you can. Next, say the prayer with focus your intent and expectation:

Ancient spirits of the Light,

Help me manifest this night.

My goals are sacred unto me,

Help me banish blocks which I may not see.

All stops that are in my goals way,

Take them all instantly away.

Thank you spirits. Amen

Proper Candle: Yellow or brown or black

Proper Incense: Magnet or hyacinth

Proper Day: Thursday

* * * * *

PRAYER FOR MONEY

Money is energy in a different form. Think of it as part of the barter system.

The better you do, the more freedom you have. You have free time to help others or to do the things you would like to do that makes you happy. We are supposed to be happy. God does not want us to suffer.

Say this prayer with conviction and expectancy:

Money, money flow to me,

Come easily and readily.

I am the magnet that attracts,

Cosmic law does now demand.

Thank you Divine Power. And it is so. Amen

Proper Candle: Green or orange

Proper Incense: Cinnamon or jasmine

Proper Day: Sunday or Thursday

* * * * *

PRAYER FOR SUCCESS

Success comes in many variations. Sometimes it is financial, or to do with health, business, finding a job, higher energy, marriage and so much more.

When you work with this prayer, make sure you focus on the area that you want the success in. If you do not have a particular area then let it go wherever it will. If you have several, you can focus on all of them as long as you can truly keep focused on your intents.

Pray:

Through Divine Power, in a perfect way,

Success comes to me in every way.

Through dark of night, through sunny days,

Success is mine without delay.

Amen

Proper Candle: Gold candle

Proper Incense: Success or High John The Conqueror

Proper Day: Sunday

* * * * *

PRAYER FOR PROPHETIC DREAMS

We all have dreams. It is our natural way to work through what happened in our day, our problems, and our happy experiences.

We are not limited by time and space in this situation and so can see the future as well as the present and what happened in our past. Sometimes we solve problems in our dream state, at times it doesn't have any specific purpose.

To consciously utilize this ability, go to bed with a pen and paper to write down your dreams immediately upon awakening.

Then say this prayer as you are ready to doze off and repeat three times:

Dreams of future yet to be,

Let me see what you hold for me.

Make it clear and make it dramatic,

So I remember my futures' fantastic.

If I should see what I do not like,

In my dreams I will change its flight.

But if I see a future pleasing

I will leave it forming clearly.

Proper Candle: Purple

Proper Incense: Rose or jasmine

Proper Day: Monday

* * * * *

PRAYER FOR PROBLEMS AT WORK

We all have situations where we deal with disgruntled co-workers on a job or just people who are negative in general or situations that are problematic.

Pray this prayer:

Chaos that is everywhere,

Take flight away from me.

Help me to clearly see,

How negative energies do not follow me.

As the sun moves in the sky,

So my energy raises high.

Chaos leaves and calmness rises,

My place of work is now more joyous.

So be it.

Proper Candle: Purple

Proper Incense: Violet or High John or sage

Proper Date: Thursday

* * * * *

PRAYER FOR THANKS

We should always say thanks for any prayers that were answered. It is so we acknowledge we were helped by Divine Power and to keep the circle / the flow going for the next time we have the need to call on prayer.

And so we pray:

I now thank Divine Power for the help and intercession that came on my behalf.

The help to make it through each day. The help that I know is always there. I know that as I ask, I am already answered and would like to take this moment to say thank you from my heart with sincerity.

Thank you Lord. Amen

Proper Candle: Violet or white

Proper Incense: Sandalwood or rose or lily

Proper Day: Every day

* * * * *

PETITIONS AND PRAYERS

Create in Me a Pure Heart

Bahá'u'lláh

Create in me a pure heart, O my God,
And renew a tranquil conscience within me, O my Hope!
Through the spirit of power confirm Thou me in Thy Cause,
O my Best-Beloved,
And by the light of Thy glory reveal unto me Thy path,
O Thou the Goal of my desire!
Through the power of Thy transcendent might
Lift me up unto the heaven of Thy holiness,
O Source of my being,
And by the breezes of Thine eternity gladden me,
O Thou Who art my God!
Let Thine everlasting melodies breathe tranquillity on me,
O my Companion,
And let the riches of Thine ancient countenance
Deliver me from all except Thee, O my Master,
And let the tidings of the revelation of Thine
Incorruptible Essence bring me joy,
O Thou Who art the most manifest of the manifest
And the most hidden of the hidden!

Candle—Dark Blue
Incense—Tobacco
Day—Thursday

All the Workers

John Baillie

O Lord, I remember before thee tonight all the workers of the world:

Workers with hand or brain:

Workers in cities or in the fields:

Men who go forth to toil and women who keep house:

Employers and employees: Those who command and those who obey:

Those whose work is dangerous:

Those whose work is monotonous or mean:

Those who can find no work to do:

Those whose work is in the service of the poor

Or healing the sick

Or the proclamation of the gospel of Christ

At home or in foreign places.

Candle—Blue
Incense—Sage and Lavender
Day—Monday

Serenity Prayer

God grant me the serenity to accept the things I cannot change; courage to change the things I can; and wisdom to know the difference.

Living one day at a time; enjoying one moment at a time; accepting hardships as the pathway to peace; taking, as He did, this sinful world as it is, not as I would have it; trusting that He will make all things right if I surrender to His Will; that I may be reasonably happy in this life and supremely happy with Him forever in the next.

Amen.

Candle—White
Incense—Sage
Day—Sunday

Think on These Things

Philippians 4
Whatsoever things are true,
Whatsoever things are honorable,
Whatsoever things are just,
Whatsoever things are pure,
Whatsoever things are lovely,
Whatsoever things are of good report;
If there be any virtue,
And if there be any praise,
Think on these things.

Candle—Red
Incense—Lemon
Day—Wednesday

Prayer for Hearing God's Word

Jim & Kaye Johns

Father, I'm praying for (name one or more) and others in my circle of family and friends who need Christ...

You are the God who gives life to the spiritually dead. (Romans 4:17b)

I thank You that everyone who calls on the name of the Lord will be saved. But Scripture asks, How can these I'm praying for call on Jesus if they have not believed in Him? And how can they believe in Him if they've not heard about Him? And how can they hear without someone bringing the truth to them? And how can they hear unless that person is sent? (Romans 10:13–15a)

I ask You to send someone into each of their lives, someone with the message of life, the Word of Christ—for Your Word does not return empty; it accomplishes what You desire and achieves the purpose for which it is sent. (Romans 10:17; Isaiah 55:11)

May they hear the words of Christ, for His words are spirit and they are life. May the words that they hear not be stolen from their hearts. (John 6:63; Luke 8:12)

Send someone they can respect to bring them the truth. In Jesus' name, amen.

Candle—Blue
Incense—Sage
Day—Tuesday

Refresh and Gladden My Spirit

Abdu'l-Bahá

O God! Refresh and gladden my spirit. Purify my heart. Illumine my powers.

I lay all my affairs in Thy hand. Thou art my Guide and my Refuge. I will no longer be sorrowful and grieved; I will be a happy and joyful being.

O God! I will no longer be full of anxiety, nor will I let trouble harass me. I will not dwell on the unpleasant things of life.

O God! Thou art more friend to me than I am to myself. I dedicate myself to Thee, O Lord.

Candle—Lavender or White
Incense—Cedarwood
Day—Monday

To Love One Another
Jim & Kaye Johns
Father, I'm praying for myself and all those in my immediate and extended family (name them)...

Help us love each other as we love ourselves. May the Holy Spirit, who has poured Your love into our hearts, give us Your selfless love, for our love falls far short of the mark. (Matthew 22:39; Romans 5:5)

May those who are married have Your perfect love especially for each other and their children. May every child be considered as Your reward, to be loved and nurtured and taught how to live lives that are obedient and pleasing to You. May we as a family be united in love. (Galatians 5:22a; Psalm 127:3; Ephesians 6:4b; 1 John 3:21–22; Colossians 2:2a)

May we submit ourselves to one another—considering others more important than ourselves, putting the others' interests ahead of our own. Help us to treat each other the way we would want to be treated in every circumstance. (Ephesians 5:21; Philippians 2:3b–4; Matthew 7:12)

May our relationships be built on these principles—for if they are, what could ever come between us? You always know what's best!

In Jesus' name, amen.

Candle—Pink
Incense—Rose
Day—Friday

Be Generous in Prosperity

Be generous in prosperity,
And thankful in adversity.

Be fair in judgment,
And guarded in speech.

Be a lamp unto those,
Who walk in darkness.

Be eyes to the blind,
And a guiding light.

Be a breath of life,
To the body of mankind.

Be a dew to the soul
Of the human heart.

And a fruit upon the tree,
Of humanity.

Candle—Gold
Incense—Sage
Day—Sunday

Prayer for the Homeless

Vienna Cobb Anderson

O God, as Naomi and Ruth journeyed from one land to another seeking a home, we ask your blessing upon all who are homeless in this world. You promised to your chosen people a land flowing with milk and honey; so inspire us to desire the accomplishment of your will that we may work for the settlement of those who are homeless in a place of peace, protection, and nurture, flowing with opportunity, blessing, and hope. Amen.

Candle—Orange
Incense—Lemon Grass
Day—Monday

Prayer for Renewal

Psalms 51: 9-12

Hide Your face from my sins, and blot out all my iniquities. Create in me a clean heart, O God, and renew a steadfast spirit within me. Do not cast me away from Your presence, and do not take Your Holy Spirit from me. Restore to me the joy of Your salvation, and uphold me by Your generous Spirit.

Candle—Purple
Incense—Pine
Day—Sunday

Prayer for Freedom From Suffering
The Buddha
May all beings everywhere plagued
with sufferings of body and mind
quickly be freed from their illnesses.
May those frightened cease to be afraid,
and may those bound be free.
May the powerless find power,
and may people think of befriending
one another.
May those who find themselves in trackless,
fearful wilderness—
the children, the aged, the unprotected—
be guarded by beneficent celestials,
and may they swiftly attain Buddhahood.

Candle—White
Incense—Frankincense
Day—Saturday

With Every Breath
Anonymous
With every breath I take today,
I vow to be awake;

And every step I take,
I vow to take with a grateful heart—

So I may see with eyes of love
into the hearts of all I meet,

To ease their burden when I can
And touch them with a smile of peace.

Candle—Purple
Incense—Rose
Day—Thursday

Prayer for Peace
Anonymous
Eternal God, in whose perfect kingdom no sword is drawn but the sword of righteousness, no strength known but the strength of love: So mightily spread abroad your spirit, that all peoples may be gathered under the banner of the Prince of Peace, as children of one creator; to whom be dominion and glory, now and for ever. Amen.

Candle—Blue
Incense—Frankincense
Day—Friday

Prayer to Live With Grace
Rabbi Rami M. Shapiro
May we discover through pain and torment,
the strength to live with grace and humor.
May we discover through doubt and anguish,
the strength to live with dignity and holiness.
May we discover through suffering and fear,
the strength to move toward healing.
May it come to pass that we be restored to health and to vigor.
May Life grant us wellness of body, spirit, and mind.
And if this cannot be so, may we find in this
transformation and passage
moments of meaning, opportunities for love
and the deep and gracious calm that comes
when we allow ourselves to move on.

Candle—Pink
Incense—Rose
Day—Sunday

Give Us, O Lord, a Steadfast Heart

Thomas Aquinas

Give us, O Lord, a steadfast heart, which no unworthy affection may drag downwards; give us an unconquered heart, which no tribulation can wear out; give us an upright heart, which no unworthy purpose may tempt aside. Bestow upon us also, O Lord our God, understanding to know you, diligence to seek you, wisdom to find you, and a faithfulness that may finally embrace you; through Jesus Christ our Lord.

Candle—Pink
Incense—Rose
Day—Sunday

Prayer for All of Humanity

Beliefnet member *LadyLovelyBug*

I pray for all of humanity to one day feel the pulse of the Mother Earth in their feet as they tread. I pray for mankind to find the faith to believe in the messages carried by their dreams and to see beyond the visible world. I pray that everyone I come in contact with can walk away with much, or at least some, of the happiness that lives within me. I pray for peace, acceptance, and tolerance for all who express their love for the higher power (whatever that name may be). Most of all, I pray for an end to the violence and depravity that darkens many souls. Peace be with us all!

Candle—White
Incense—White Sage
Day—Monday

Prayer for Peace

Lord, make me an instrument of Thy peace;
where there is hatred, let me sow love;
where there is injury, pardon;
where there is doubt, faith;
where there is despair, hope;
where there is darkness, light;
and where there is sadness, joy.

O Divine Master, grant that I may not so much seek to be consoled as to console; to be understood, as to understand; to be loved, as to love; for it is in giving that we receive, it is in pardoning that we are pardoned, and it is in dying that we are born to eternal life.

Amen.

—St. Francis of Assisi (1181-1226)

Candle—White
Incense—Vanilla
Day—Monday

A Prayer to God Our Help

Our God, our help in ages past, Our hope for years to come, Our shelter from the stormy blast, And our eternal home!

Beneath the shadow of Thy throne Still may we dwell secure; Sufficient is Thine arm alone, And our defense is sure.

Before the hills in order stood, Or earth received her frame, From everlasting Thou art God, To endless years the same.

A thousand ages in Thy sight Are like an evening gone; Short as the watch that ends the night Before the rising sun.

The busy tribes of flesh and blood, With all their cares and fears, Are carried downward by the flood, And lost in following years.

Thy Word commands our flesh to dust: "Return, ye sons of men!" All nations rose from earth at first And turn to earth again.

Time, like an ever rolling stream, Bears all its sons away; They fly forgotten as a dream Dies at the opening day.

Like flowery fields the nations stand, Pleased with the morning light; The flowers beneath the mower's hand Lie withering ere 'tis night.

Our God our help in ages past, Our hope for years to come, Be Thou our guard while life shall last, And our eternal home.

—Isaac Watts, 1719

Candle—Blue
Incense—Amber
Day—Sunday

Healing Prayer

Dear Lord of Mercy and Father of Comfort,

You are the One I turn to for help in moments of weakness and times of need. I ask you to be with your servant in this illness. Psalm 107:20 says that you send out your Word and heal. So then, please send your healing Word to your servant. In the name of Jesus, drive out all infirmity and sickness from his body.

Dear Lord, I ask you to turn this weakness into strength, suffering into compassion, sorrow into joy, and pain into comfort for others. May your servant trust in your goodness and hope in your faithfulness, even in the middle of this suffering. Let him be filled with patience and joy in your presence as he waits for your healing touch.

Please restore your servant to full health, dear Father. Remove all fear and doubt from his heart by the power of your Holy Spirit, and may you, Lord, be glorified through his life.

As you heal and renew your servant, Lord, may he bless and praise you.

All of this I pray in the name of Jesus Christ.

Amen.

Candle—Green
Incense—Pine or Mint
Day—Monday

Prayer for Comfort in Loss

Dear Lord, Please help me in this time of loss and overwhelming grief. I don't understand why my life is filled with this pain and heartache. But I turn my eyes to you as I seek to find the strength to trust in your faithfulness. I will wait on you and not despair; I will quietly wait for your salvation. My heart is crushed, but I know that you will not abandon me forever. Please show me your compassion, Lord. Help me through the pain so that I will hope in you again. I believe this promise in your Word to send me fresh mercy each day. Though I can't see past today, I trust your great love will never fail me.

Amen.

Candle—White
Incense—Sanctuary or Frankincense
Day—Sunday

A MIRACLE A MINUTE
With Candle Burning Prayers For A Good And Prosperous Life

Interested parties may visit Maria D' Andrea's Web Site

http://www.mariadandrea.com/

Maria is also available for private counseling at

Mailing address: PO BOX 52 Mineola, NY 11501

Offices on Long Island and Manhattan Phone: (631) 559-1248

Email: maria@mariadandrea.com

PayPal: mdandrea100@gmail.com

Maria's Books Are Available From Her Publisher

Timothy G. Beckley

Box 753, New Brunswick, NJ 08903

646 331-6777

A MIRACLE A MINUTE
With Candle Burning Prayers For A Good And Prosperous Life

Psychic Readings
by Maria D'Andrea,
MsD, D.D., DRH

KEY TO AN ABUNDANT LIFE

Maria D'Andrea is an internationally known psychic from Budapest, Hungary. Since early childhood she has demonstrated high spiritual awareness and psychic ability. She is a professional psychic, published author, Spiritual Life Coach, metaphysician, public speaker and lecturer, European Shaman , Founder of several organizations, and is frequent in the media scene, among other disciplines.

Maria is tuned in between the two worlds of man and Divine Power to access information so you can be empowered to achieve abundance and success in all areas of your life such as:

- **Career:** To guide you to an abundant, secure career
- **Romance:** To help you to improve your life and to make the correct decisions for yourself
- **Decisions:** To make them to your benefit, in a positive, abundant way

Think of psychic information as you being on one end of a phone call, Divine Power on the other end and Maria as being the wire that connects you, through her ability to enter an altered state of mind at will.

Rune Casting is an ancient, pre-Bronze Age, European system which is a trigger for psychic information. Utilized for centuries by shaman, magi and others to bring forth the information for you to create an abundant life.

Maria utilizes this system and other disciplines to help you to a life of abundance and to answer any questions you may have.

BOOK BY MARIA D'ANDREA

Secret Occult Gallery And Spell Casting Formulary

Your Personal Mega Power Spells - For Love, Luck, Prosperity

Curses And Their Reversals - Plus: Omens, Superstitions And The Removal Of The Evil Eye

Occult Grimoire And Magical Formulary: A Workbook For Creating A Positive Life

How To Eliminate Stress And Anxiety Through The Occult:

Secret Magical Elixirs Of Life

Heaven Sent Money Spells

Mystical, Magickal Beasts And Beings

* * * * *

*Available From Amazon.Com world wide
or Fishpond in NZ and Australia*

*Or direct from the publisher
Timothy G. Beckley
mrufo8@hotmail.com*